10 Years
of
Excellence

Chase Reynolds Ewald

2002 SOURCEBOOK

Front cover:
Photo: Elijah Cobb

Back Cover:
Piece by Lester Santos
Santos Furniture,
Cody, Wyoming
Photo: Elijah Cobb

Inside Front Cover:
Photo: Dewey Vanderhoff

Inside Back Cover:
Photo: Dewey Vanderhoff

The Western Design Conference Sourcebook
2002

Writer
Chase Reynolds Ewald

Editors
Gwen Fordham
Executive Assistant
Pamela K. Neary
Executive Director

Photos: Dewey Vanderhoff

Fashion Show Producer
Christie Shook

*The Western Design Conference
is supported in part by grants from
the Cody Economic Development Council
and the City of Cody, Wyoming.*

Published by
Pronghorn Press, Shell, Wyoming

For

The Western Design Institute
Cody, Wyoming
888-685-0574
website: www.wdcinfo.org
email: gwen@wdcinfo.org

Writer: Chase Reynolds Ewald • Editors: Pamela K. Neary & Gwen Fordham
Book Design: Antelope Design, Shell, Wyoming • Color Reproductions: Scan West, Missoula, Montana

Library of Congress Number 2002105838

Soft Cover ISBN 0-9676662-3-6 • Hard Cover ISBN 0-9676662-4-4

Table of Contents

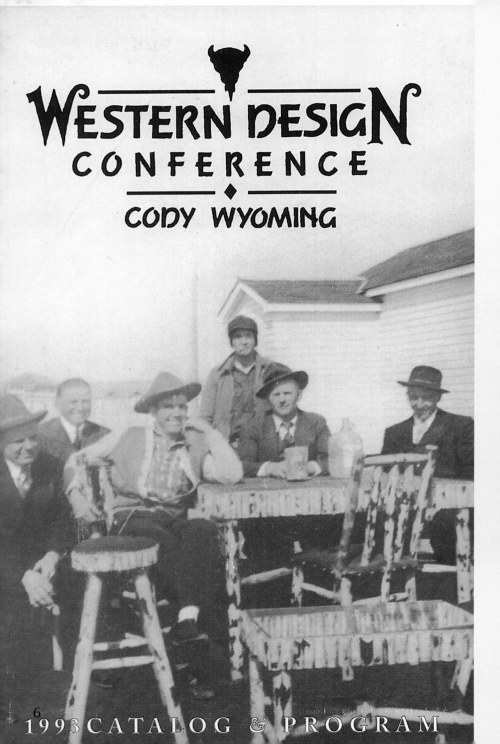

WESTERN DESIGN
CONFERENCE
• CODY WYOMING •

10 Years of Excellence

by Chase Reynolds Ewald

A decade has passed since a pioneering group of Western Design enthusiasts — furnituremakers, traditional artisans, fashion designers, museum curators, architects, interior designers, western homeowners, authors, publishers, and magazine editors — gathered in Cody for the first official Western Design Conference. The excitement was palpable that September, from the keynote address by author/designer Mary Emmerling at Cody's Art Deco movie theater, to the buzz surrounding the thirty exhibitors' booths that filled the old Cody Auditorium, to the sold-out fashion show, held the last night of the conference in a 100-year-old barn at historic Trail Town.

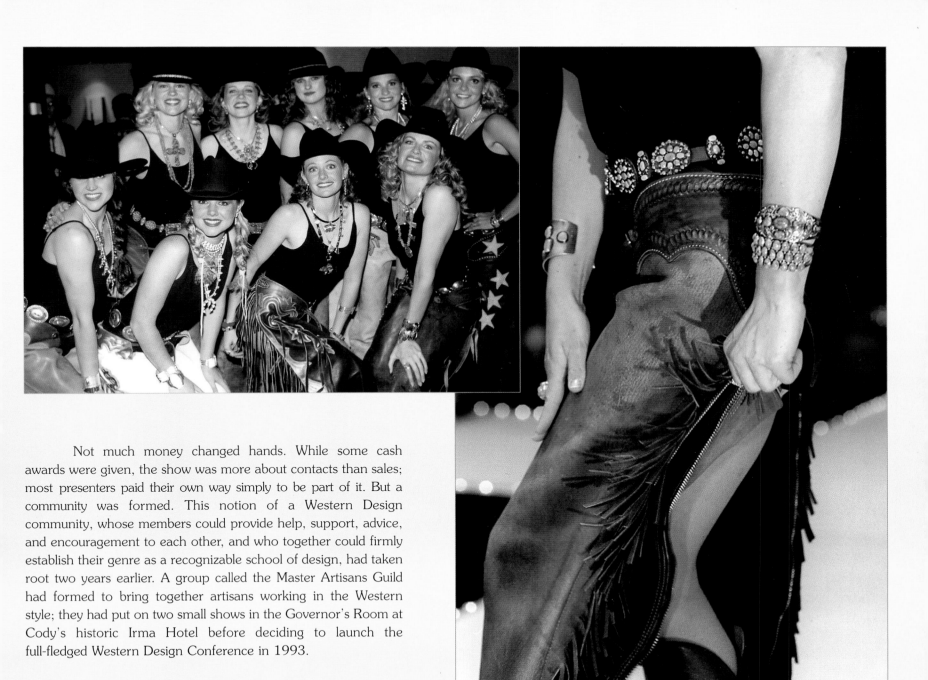

Not much money changed hands. While some cash awards were given, the show was more about contacts than sales; most presenters paid their own way simply to be part of it. But a community was formed. This notion of a Western Design community, whose members could provide help, support, advice, and encouragement to each other, and who together could firmly establish their genre as a recognizable school of design, had taken root two years earlier. A group called the Master Artisans Guild had formed to bring together artisans working in the Western style; they had put on two small shows in the Governor's Room at Cody's historic Irma Hotel before deciding to launch the full-fledged Western Design Conference in 1993.

From the first, the Conference was a sensation, from the pole-and-leather furniture on the exhibition floor to the beadwork-and-fringe outfits sashaying down the fashion show runway. As then-Governor of Wyoming, Mike Sullivan later wrote, "The Conference put to rest the notion that Western style is not a fad, but a trend which continues to grow, and for some of us is simply a part of our background and heritage that we've always loved and appreciated. The success of the first annual Conference was no surprise to the people involved. But they didn't anticipate the enormous turnout in support of Western style and design."

In the ensuing decade, the Conference has evolved, both in terms of format and in terms of the quality and diverse stylistic influences in the work being presented. Although the Conference has always been comprised of the same elements that it has today —

Left: Chris Chapman

Artisans enjoying the opportunity to meet and converse.

Right: Lester Santos and David Struempler

a furniture and functional-art exhibition, a fashion show, and educational seminars — its format has changed, and with it, the quality of each individual work. Originally a word-of-mouth show with the work shown in decorated booths, only a couple of years had passed before applicants were being selected through a blind-juried process, and the format had changed to a gallery setting. Longtime participants agree that this was the change that really drove the quality for which the Western Design Conference is now renowned. With each chair or table or pair of cowboy boots standing alone on a bare pedestal, suddenly the back was as important as the front, joinery mattered as much as design, and the quality of the stitching or finish work could make or break an artist's reputation.

9

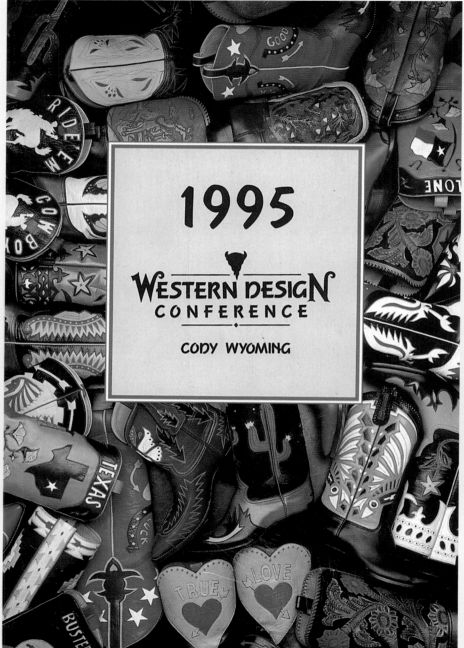

1995

WESTERN DESIGN
CONFERENCE

CODY WYOMING

Within only a few years of its founding, the Western Design Conference had established a name and earned a reputation for being the place to find museum-quality, one-of-a-kind functional-art pieces, work that expresses both a reverence for the traditions of the region while simultaneously embracing the changing West. Consequently, participation has grown considerably, with each succeeding year attracting more applicants, more participants, and greater media coverage. Five years after the founding of the Western Design Conference, 120 applicants were vying for 60 spaces. In the past five years, attendance has increased 100%. Today, fourteen awards with a combined value of $20,000 drive this continuing evolution of design and pursuit of quality. A constant influx of new talent helps keep the work fresh, while the steady commitment of long-time exhibitors, supporters and award-winners maintains the WDC's most striking characteristic: its sense of community. More than anything else, the bonds which were forged in those early years have only strengthened, while a warm western welcome continues to be extended to newcomers.

Plans for the future include an addition to the tried-and-true format; a carefully critiqued trade show will be added to offer more opportunities for Western craftspeople to display their work, and to provide more art for visitors to see. The Western Design Conference has come a long way, from a volunteer-driven effort run out the offices of New West Furniture, to a professionally run organization whose reach is international. Yet it still remains true to its initial vision: to present work that celebrates the contemporary West while paying homage to its traditions, its history, its landscapes, and its ways of life.

Photo: Dewey Vanderhoff

Cody, Wyoming

The past is always present in Buffalo Bill's Yellowstone Country. This corner of northwest Wyoming is the true West, a place where cowboy culture thrives but where traditional culture is just as vital. The country is rugged, the people genuine and the opportunities for adventure and relaxation are nearly endless. This is not the West of Hollywood. This is the real West. We take our history seriously. It's all around us, all the time.

If you are searching for a taste of the real American West, Cody, Wyoming is a good place to start. The city was founded in 1896 by the most authentic representative of the Old West, Colonel, William F. "Buffalo Bill" Cody.

Buffalo Bill lived up to the romantic idea of the brave, daring frontiersman. Through his personal exploits and his Wild West Show he became the world's most well known American. It is his name which represents the true epitome of the Old West, and has provided a draw to this small western town, where real cowboys still herd cattle and buffalo still roam.

Cody is home to the largest history and art museum between Minneapolis and the West Coast, encompassing 300,000 square feet. Visitors to the Buffalo Bill Historical Center are often stunned to find such an immense storehouse of Western history and art in a town with a population of just 9,000.

Just 50 miles west of Cody lies the east entrance to the Nation's oldest National Park, Yellowstone. Yellowstone offers visitors a glimpse into the West as it was before the advent of settlers, railroads and highways. Visitors from all over the globe come to experience Yellowstone's geology. They come to see the huge variety of wildlife: grizzlies, gray wolves, and herds of buffalo, elk and deer. Anglers try to outwit the inhabitants of the park's trout streams. Yellowstone is immense and varied. Its wonders are accessible to everyone, young and old.

Cody, recognized as the Rodeo Capitol of the World, has featured the Cody Nite Rodeo for over 50 years. The nightly performances, from June through August, include riding, roping, and bull and bronc riding on some of the finest stock in the country featuring some of the top athletes both human and animal on the professional circuit. The Cody Stampede held each year over the 4th of July has been voted "Best Large Outdoor Rodeo" two years in a row by the Professional Cowboys Association.

With its panoramic views, Old West feel and delightful history, Cody is an unexpected treasure to thousands of travelers each year. Come and see for yourself.

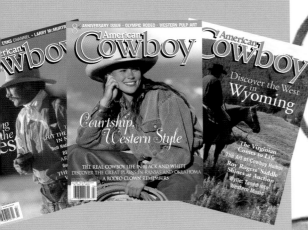

FROM THE GOVERNOR:

Welcome, to Cody, Wyoming and the Western Design Conference! As Governor of Wyoming, I am pleased to host you in our great state while showcasing the pioneering spirit that created western-style design.

I am honored to host this one-of-a kind conference in Wyoming, now celebrating "Ten Years of Excellence." What started out as a small, two-day show with 12 exhibitors at the Irma Hotel, has now grown into the Western Design Conference of today, with over 75 craftsmen and designers whose work influences western culture & design worldwide.

The authentic western-style design in furniture and decorative arts has always been a part of our lives in Wyoming. While the people of the West take great pride in the heritage that inspired western design, we applaud the artisans and craftspeople who fashion and market these designs, transforming our heritage into enterprise. The Western Design Conference provides a unique forum for the artisan and patron to showcase and exchange the latest in contemporary western decorative art, crafts, clothing and furniture.

The Western Design Conference is a tribute and celebration of the West as it once was and the designs in which it is immortalized. During your stay, take time to visit the Wyoming that inspired much of the design celebrated here. Best wishes for an enjoyable, productive and creative conference!

Best Regards,

Jim Geringer
Governor

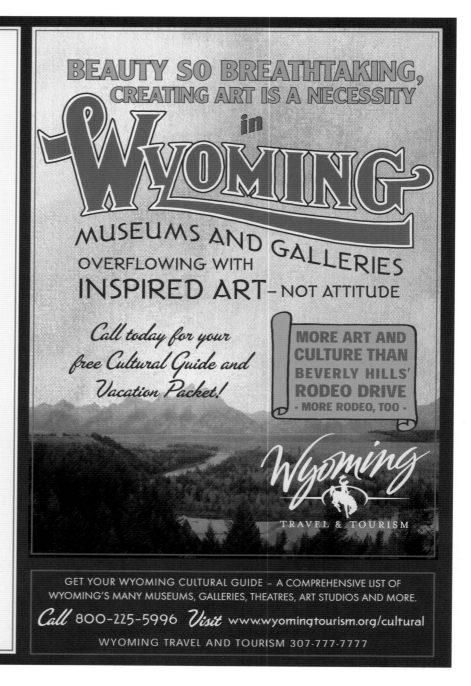

History. Mystery. Legends & Lore.

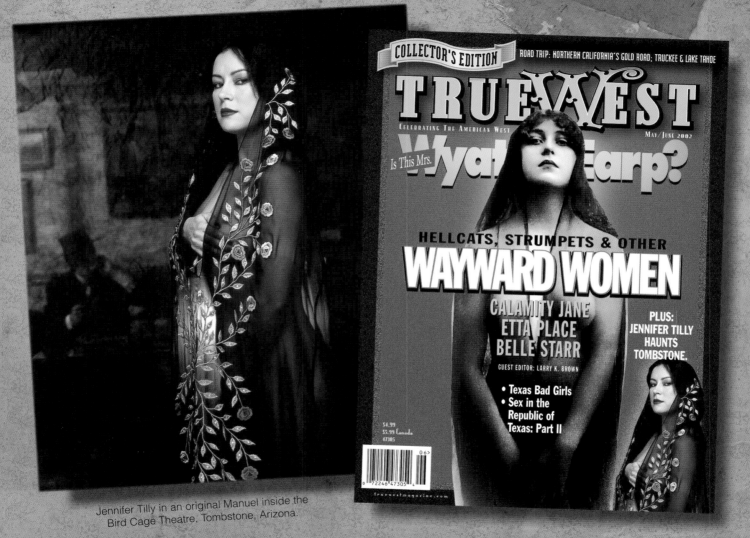

Jennifer Tilly in an original Manuel inside the
Bird Cage Theatre, Tombstone, Arizona.

COLLECTOR'S EDITION ROAD TRIP: NORTHERN CALIFORNIA'S GOLD ROAD; TRUCKEE & LAKE TAHOE

TRUE WEST
CELEBRATING THE AMERICAN WEST
MAY/JUNE 2002

Is This Mrs. **Wyatt Earp?**

HELLCATS, STRUMPETS & OTHER
WAYWARD WOMEN

CALAMITY JANE
ETTA PLACE
BELLE STARR

GUEST EDITOR: LARRY K. BROWN

PLUS:
JENNIFER TILLY
HAUNTS
TOMBSTONE.

• Texas Bad Girls
• Sex in the
  Republic of
  Texas: Part II

$4.99
$5.99 Canada
47305

truewestmagazine.com

What else do you want in a Western magazine?

TRUE WEST

Celebrating the American West since 1953.

www.truewestmagazine.com • toll free 888-687-1881

Inside Cody are more than 4,000 works of art.

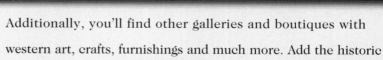

It's rather fitting that the Western Design Conference is in Cody, Wyoming. After all, in Cody, all directions point west. Cody was founded by the man largely responsible for popularizing western life and art through his Wild West Show: Buffalo Bill Cody. So it should come as no surprise that today Cody is what many consider the center of the western design world. For instance, the Buffalo Bill Historical Center is the premier museum of its kind; in fact, it has been hailed as "the Smithsonian of the West."

Additionally, you'll find other galleries and boutiques with western art, crafts, furnishings and much more. Add the historic downtown, Trail Town Museum, Cody Nite Rodeo throughout the summer...well, you get the idea. If it's in the

Outside are the 3 million acres that inspired them.

west, it's definitely in Cody. And let's not forget that Mother Nature has some stunning artwork of her own surrounding Cody; you'll find scenic vistas filled with mountains and wildlife all around you. Plus, if the wonders of the Cody area aren't enough for your eyes, Yellowstone National Park is just a few miles up the road. Due west, of course.

P.O. Box 2454-WDR02, 836 Sheridan
Cody, WY 82414 • 800-393-2639
www.codycountry.org

MAY
4	**Powell** • Mayfest
11-12	**Cody** • Cody Wild West Days
25	**Cody** • 5th Annual Peace Run/Rally

JUNE
1	**Cody** • Cody Nite Rodeo Begins
4	**Cody** • Opening of the Draper Museum of Natural History
6-9	**Cody** • Cowboy Action Shoot
12-16	**Ralston** • Ralston Rendezvous and Mule Days
14-16	**Cody** • 27th Annual Winchester Gun Show
15-16	**Cody** • 21st Annual Plains Indian Powwow
19	**Cody** • 13th Annual Original Cody Old West Show & Auction
20-22	**Cody** • 13th Annual Old West Show & Auction

JULY
1-4	**Cody** • 83rd Annual Cody Stampede
12-13	**Cody** • 15th Annual Yellowstone Jazz Festival

AUGUST
14-17	**Cody** • Sierracade Motorcycle Rally
15-17	**Cody** • Buffalo Bill Invitational Shootout
17	**Powell** • Wings N' Wheels

SEPTEMBER
1-2	**Meeteetse** • Annual Labor Day Celebration
5-8	**Powell** • All American Quilt Show
18	**Cody** • Western Design Conference Fashion Show
19-20	**Cody** • Annual Western Design Conference
20-21	**Cody** • Buffalo Bill Art Show & Sale

17

SEE A NEW
BUFFALO BILL
HISTORICAL CENTER

Sitting Bull and Buffalo Bill, taken in 1885 by Notman, copied by. D. F. Barry. Buffalo Bill Historical Center. P.69.2125

Before June 4th of this year, the Buffalo Bill Historical Center was an internationally renowned institution that collected, preserved, and interpreted a world-class collection of Buffalo Bill memorabilia, western art, Plains Indian arts and culture, and firearms.

THE BUFFALO BILL MUSEUM housed the story of William F. "Buffalo Bill" Cody, focusing on Buffalo Bill's worldwide career with his Wild West show. The collections also interpreted the history of the American cowboy, dude ranching, western conservation, and frontier entrepreneurship.

THE WHITNEY GALLERY OF WESTERN ART was a display of the finest western artists of the 19th Century and beyond with masterpieces by George Catlin, Alfred Jacob Miller, Thomas Moran, Albert Bierstadt, Frederic Remington, C.M. Russell, W. H. D. Koerner, N. C. Wyeth, Harry Jackson and more. You even found a wonderful collection of contemporary western art.

THE PLAINS INDIAN MUSEUM, newly reinterpreted and dedicated in 2000, explored the culture and artistry of the Plains Indian people, tracing their lives from their buffalo hunting past to the living traditions of the present.

THE CODY FIREARMS MUSEUM housed over 5,000 firearms dating back to the 16th century. Embellished, hunting, military and specialty arms suffused the museum with what has become an astounding collection and is the world's most important assemblage of American firearms.

THE MCCRACKEN RESEARCH LIBRARY included historic photographic prints and negatives as well as books, manuscript collections, and the Yale Western Americana microfilm.

18

THEN CAME THE DRAPER

On June 4th, the Buffalo Bill Historical Center changed its footprint forever. June 4th, the Center unveiled the Draper Museum of Natural History. Thanks to the generosity of philanthropist Nancy-Carroll Draper and many other donors, this 55,000 square foot addition to an already magnificent complex of museums brings the world of natural science to Cody and the study of the Greater Yellowstone region to the world.

A NEW MUSEUM FOR A NEW CENTURY

Even more significant, the Draper Museum of Natural History is on the leading edge of an international trend, examining the complex relationships between humans and nature. You enter the Draper through the *Expedition Trailhead* where you find out how and why people have explored nature through time. You follow the Trailhead to the dramatic overlook in the grand rotunda that reveals the multi-level *Mountains–to–Plains* expedition trail spiraling down before you.

You descend from alpine through mountain forest, mountain meadow, and plains environments on your way to view the dramatic T. D. Kelsey sculpture "Free Fall," depicting three 1.25 life-size scale bison tumbling over a cliff. Those sculptures are the first of more than a dozen bronze bison leading up to the exterior of the Draper. Families will especially enjoy the multimedia presentations and hands-on activities in the Draper's *Seasons of Discovery*.

This brief description just barely scratches the surface of the Draper Museum of Natural History, funded in part by the National Science Foundation. The $17 million installation is a major undertaking that increased the Buffalo Bill Historical Center's size by more than 20%.

IMMERSE YOURSELF IN THE AMERICAN WEST

Be sure to see the Buffalo Bill Historical Center while you are in Cody the week of September 16th. It is five magnificent museums with almost seven acres of western cultural and natural history. The Western Design Conference, highlighted by the annual fashion show, excites the imagination. The Buffalo Bill Art Show and Sale, the same week, showcases the very best in contemporary art of the West. The Patrons Ball, a black-tie, fund-raising dinner and dance, is the social highpoint of this week we call "Rendezvous Royale."

If you love the histories that colored the West, the heroes that peopled the West, the art and design inspired by the West, and the landscape and wildlife that continue to define the West, be in Cody in September to celebrate the past, present, and future of this spectacular region of the world.

C. R. Preston photos.

the five museums of
THE BUFFALO BILL HISTORICAL CENTER
720 Sheridan Avenue • Cody, WY • 82414 • www.bbhc.org • 307.587.4771

19

At Play in the Art of the West

by *Chase Reynolds Ewald*

Five years ago, the judges for the Western Design Conference found themselves in a quandary. The judging for the event's many prestigious awards was as tough as ever. But now there was a new phenomenon to grapple with: a number of contenders in a category for which no award existed.

Thom Ross and Tim Groth's *Wild Bench"* was a beautifully crafted leather upholstered wooden bench with twisted and curved juniper legs and multi-hued applied-pole detail. Its back incorporated a life-size image of Butch Cassidy and the Sundance Kid's Hole in the Wall Gang; five men dressed in their Sunday best: three-piece suits, watch chains visible, derby hats perched aloft. Pat Olson had created *Neon Dream* a table whose base was a multi-layered sculpture of a cowgirl made from metal sheets. The girl, cowboy hat cocked back, was holding a beer bottle and leaning back, one elbow resting on the glass top of the table in a classic bar pose. There were several other entries combining the same high levels of craftsmanship and originality, and a similarly offbeat sense of fun.

Recalls interior designer Hilary Heminway, who served as a judge that year: "We saw some very seriously beautiful things; there was some beautiful craftsmanship, and some of them had a fabulous sense of humor. Your tendency, when you pick Best of Show, or a piece for a museum collection, is to go for something serious and straightforward with beautiful craftsmanship. Here were these things that had a sense of humor, but still had the same quality."

1997 Best Western Spirit Award Winner, *The Wild Bench*
Thom Ross & Tim Groth, Boise, Idaho

The judges were successful in prevailing upon the conference administrators to simply create a new award. Hence was born the Best Western Spirit Award, which celebrates the West's unique sense of humor and appreciation for whimsy — and its ability to confront difficult situations with a wry smile.

"So many of the hardships and adversities in the West have been saved by humor," says Hilary Heminway, whose own contributions to the field of Western design have included a Westernized Airstream trailer, a Zen meditation house, and an award-winning designer outhouse. "You see it in poetry, in music, in paintings. It's like saying, 'If we take ourselves not quite so seriously we may survive this.' So I think this work is made with that in mind."

Mike Patrick, a fourth-generation Cody rancher, furnituremaker and co-founder of the Western Design Conference explains, "The level of pretension is lower here, so you can laugh at yourself a little bit." Besides, as a ranch kid growing up, he recalls, "Being around real, honest-to-goodness cowhands and ranch workers, you learned not to take yourself too seriously. They would deflate you in an instant with just a comment or a joke."

This is not to say one can't make a serious statement with a seemingly humorous piece of furniture. Patrick's irrigation bed — built from shovels, an aluminum half-wheel, sprinklers, and some gated pipe and fittings from different types of irrigation systems — was not meant to be outrageous, he insists. It speaks, he says, to the true West.

"The West was not about gunfights. It was about neighbors helping neighbors. Without that, they wouldn't have survived. Anyone who has studied the subject soon realizes that 'winning the West' was ultimately a matter of controlling and manipulating water. In spite of the literature in the early part of this century, or Hollywood's later projected reality, it was not the "Indian Wars" or cattle drives and ranching that were decisive in the white mans' ascendancy. The palette that painted the West was water."

Pat's Pull Toy
Pat Olson's Sculpture & Furniture Art
Photo: Herb Sanders

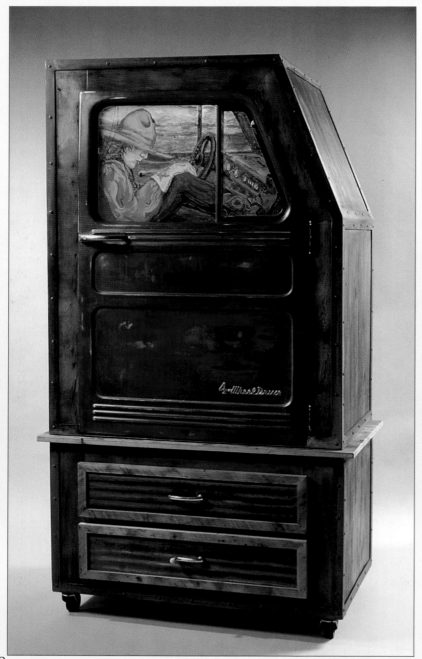

This furniture may challenge our notions of history, as with Patrick's water bed, or it may explore the very concept of perception, as in the work of Colorado artisan, Pat Olson. His sculpture-like pieces, made from layers of steel, appear to be whimsical or even humorous, but raise as many questions as they answer. A horse sculpture, for instance, is made into a rolling table with two overlapped sheets of glass for its top and large gold discs cutout with horse shapes for its wheels. "The style of the work, layers of two-dimensional stainless steel sheets arranged to make recognizable three-dimensional figures, is a subtle reminder of the saying that things are not always the way they appear," explains the artist. "Point of view has a great deal to do with one's understanding."

Western-spirited furniture is historically minded while remaining forward-looking. Consequently, the use of reclaimed materials in often contemporary-looking pieces plays a big part in Western design, whether it's an elegant home incorporating old railroad timbers or a barstool made from a rusty tractor seat. Idaho craftsman Dana Merrill uses only recycled products in his furniture: richly patinaed wood from his neighbors' abandoned barns, rusty nails, harness rings, bits, tobacco cans, and old leather reins. "Self-reliance is a very important part of Western thought," says Merrill, who grew up on the ranches of his grandfather and thirteen aunts and uncles. "Even for the new Westerners, people from the East come here looking for that romance. Reusing what you have and trying to make do is important."

Wyoming artisan Lynn Arambel is always inspired by old things, from picket fences to pickle vats. In 2000, she designed an entertainment center around a pickup truck door. The door of the 1949 Willys, finally discovered in an auto salvage yard after much searching, bears the words "4-Wheel Drive" in 1940's script in its lower corner and its original handle. You can still roll down the window, which has been painted with an image of a cowgirl, her cowboy-booted foot up against the dashboard, gauntlet gloved-hand resting on

Lynn Seder Arambel, Ranch Willow Furniture
Sheridan, Wyoming   Photo: Elijah Cobb

knee, cowboy hat tipped down, as she snoozes in the cab of the pickup. Visible through the far window is a vista of plains, with mountains in the distance. With the window rolled down, the viewer has a perfect view of the 19" television screen resting on the top shelf. The leather panel on the inside of the door, handcrafted by a leather worker from King Saddle shop in Sheridan, Wyoming, bears entertainment "brands" like "DVD," "TV," and "VCR," interspersed with real brands from neighboring ranches.

"I like the idea of giving things another life," says Arambel. "With things that are old, particularly wooden things, there was a lot of labor that went into what people did back then. It wasn't done by a computerized machine. It was labor-intensive, and the work has more character."

Greg Race often incorporates industrial artifacts into his decidedly contemporary but still very Western pieces. He built an award-winning cocktail table from a large industrial gear, which he inset with glass, and used spoke-like metal pieces for its legs. "As a design medium," he says, "found objects provide a level of depth and sophistication that cannot be replicated using new raw materials. Old materials have a history, style, and feel that, when implemented into a finished piece of furniture, are intrinsically complex and inviting."

Says Hilary Heminway, whose own work makes creative use of old materials, "Using bits and pieces of things that are salvaged is another aspect of

the spirit of the West. People lived 100 miles from the nearest town. They had to be creative, and they had to make do."

Most artisans get their inspiration from the West itself — its timeless scenery and traditional lifestyles — whether they're on the road or working around the ranch. "I get visions of things when I'm driving by myself," says Lynn Arambel. "I get a lot of my colors when I'm driving, from the fields. I feel really blessed because it comes naturally to me; I'm not fighting all the time for ideas."

For Oregon designer Anne Beard, "A ranch upbringing, life on

Best Artist, Metal 2000
Stray Horse Standard Cocktail Table Set
Quandary Designs, Leadville, Colorado
Photo: Todd Powell

the high desert, and continued exposure to the Beard family business of PRCA rodeo stock contracting, infuse my work with Western spirit." In the marriage of couturier work and furniture-making, Beard has developed the concept of "furniture wearing clothes." Her *Cowgirl Cameo* ottoman of brown and red wool gabardine, (which won the *Best Western Spirit* award in 1998), is decorated with appliqued horseshoes and tassels of twisted doeskin. On top is a "cameo" of a cowgirl with her horse. Tucked underneath the skirt is a leather strip bearing the words, 'As sure as there are stars above, we're not the first to fall in love.' Explains the artist, "It evokes universal nostalgia for all those women whose best childhood friend outweighed them by a ton. The world does indeed look different from the back of a horse."

James Ferrara, of Ferrara Design in Washington, was also inspired by "many years and thousands of miles of driving." His line of furniture called *The Fence Line* features legs made of fence posts, and panels of punched and embossed tin; each piece incorporates real tumbleweeds, stones, and a "Spanish winch," (western slang for fence tightener). Like many Western-spirited pieces, it's whimsical, it's original, and it speaks to the heart and soul of the West: in this case, big distances, a livestock-based economy, and the fence as a symbol of the taming of the frontier.

"Because the West has defined for generations of Americans what we deem to be our national character, Western design has reflected that character," says Mike Patrick. "It tends to be casual, humorous, warm, friendly, and utilitarian, and makes wonderful use of the experiences, materials, and native traditions of the West. It is essential to maintain the integrity of those elements. Rather than the hokey or glitzy elements handed to us from Hollywood, I hope Western design reinterprets the real visions of the western culture and environment."

"To me," says Hilary Heminway, "this furniture represents the spirit of the West. It's as if to say, 'Come on, pull your boots on, stand tall — and don't forget to laugh along the way!' "

10 Years of Excellence

The

WESTERN DESIGN
CONFERENCE

Awards

1997 Switchback Ranch Award Winner
Purple Sage Smoking Jacket
Anne Beard, Lexington, Oregon
Photo: DeGabrielle

25

*B*est of show

2001

The Yellowstone Desk
Norseman Designs West
John Gallis, Cody, Wyoming
Photo: Elijah Cobb

Craftsmanship, originality of design and representation of the Western genre are key factors that influence the judges when selecting the Best of Show winner. This award is a cash award sponsored by Foster and Lynn Friess of Jackson, Wyoming.

2000

Stacked Log Chair,
Vaquero Style
Wood River Rustics
Doug & Janis Tedrow
Ketchum, Idaho

1999

Executive Decision
Wildewood Furniture
Ron & Jean Shanor
Cody, Wyoming

1998

Leather Wrapped King Size Bed
Chapman Designs
Chris Chapman
Carbondale, Colorado

1997

Moose Chair
MacPhail's Studio
Dan MacPhail,
Kevil, Kentucky

1996

The Wild Absaroka Desk
Santos Furniture
Lester Santos
Cody, Wyoming

1995

Sheepwagon
Montana Wagons
Hilary Heminway & Terry Baird
McLeod, Montana

1994

Buffet
Triangle Z Ranch Furniture
Kendall Siggins
Cody, Wyoming

1993

Keeska Desk
Covert Workshops
Jim & Lynda Covert
Cody, Wyoming

Fashion
Designer of the Year

A new award in 1999, presented to the fashion designer who has made an impact on the Western couture fashion world with a collection of one-of-a-kind pieces of outstanding quality, fit and design.

2001

Rendezvous Royale
Anne Beard
Lexington, Oregon
Photos: David Wesley Vaughan

2000

Leather Legends
Marge & Tammy Taylor
Fromberg, Montana

1999

Teepee Smoke
Anne Beard
Lexington, Oregon

This award reflects the impressions of those who attend the exhibition as the public casts their own votes for their favorite piece.

Peoples' *Choice* Award

2000
Pony Express Desk III & Switchback Chair

Norseman Designs West
John Gallis
Cody, Wyoming

1999
Spirits Untamed

Amber Jean
Livingston, Montana
in collaboration with

High Country Designs
Don & Steve Butts
Frisco, Colorado

1998
Pony Express Desk

Norseman Designs West
John Gallis
Cody, Wyoming

1997
Antler Christmas Tree

MacPhail's Studios
Dan MacPhail
Kevil, Kentucky

1996
Cavalry & Indians

Triangle Z Ranch Furniture
Kendall Siggins
Cody, Wyoming

1995
New West
J. Mike Patrick
Cody, Wyoming

1994
New West
J. Mike Patrick
Cody, Wyoming

1994
Timber Creek Interiors
Cody, Wyoming

1993
Matt Mattson
Orik, California

2001
Majestic Moose Bar
Hone's Cabinet and Design
Al Hone & Teresa Hone
Benjamin, Utah

Exhibitors' *Choice*

Long considered the most prestigious award because the recipients are chosen by their peers, the Exhibitors' Choice Award is selected through secret ballot with one vote per exhibitor.

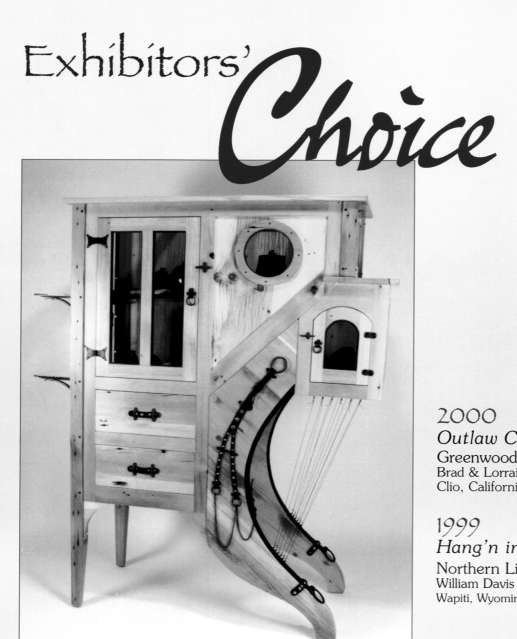

2001

Dana's Muse
R. Dana Merrill Designs
R. Dana Merrill
North Fork, Idaho
Photo: Dave Thompson

2000
Outlaw Cabinet
Greenwood Designs
Brad & Lorraine Greenwood
Clio, California

1999
Hang'n in There
Northern Lights Studio
William Davis
Wapiti, Wyoming

1998
Corral Creek Guest Desk
Covert Workshops
Jim & Lynda Covert
Cody, Wyoming

1997
Walnut Slab Desk
Norseman Designs West
John Gallis
Cody, Wyoming

This award is presented to the craftsperson whose piece is deemed exceptional in design, quality, finish and originality. The award is sponsored annually by Woodworker's Supply.

Best Woodworking
Craftsmanship

2000
End of the Trail Rocking Chair
Odell Woodworking
& Logsawing
Skip Odell
Larkspur, Colorado

1999
Pony Express Desk
Norseman Designs West
John Gallis
Cody, Wyoming

1998
Meeteetse Chest
Wood River Rustics
Doug & Janis Tedrow
Ketchum, Idaho

1997
Alpenhorn Corner Table
SweetTree Rustic
Thome George & Cloudbird
Tonasket, Washington

2001
Greenwood Designs
Brad & Lorraine Greenwood
Clio, California
Photo: Elijah Cobb

31

Best Artist *Metal*

Photo: McNabb Studio

2000

Stray Horse
Standard Cocktail Table Set
Quandary Designs
Leadville, Colorado

1999

Buffalo Sconce
Heart Mountain Forge & Design
Rik Mettes
Powell, Wyoming

1998

Fireplace Screen
Prairie Elk Forge
George Ainslie
Lavina, Montana

Art for the Hearth Fireplace Screen
Gilmore Metalsmithing Studio
Glenn Gilmore
Hamilton, Montana

2001

1997

Belt Buckle Chair
Lynn Mcevers Andrews
Cody, Wyoming

The Category Awards

These awards originated as best emerging artist awards and grew into individual category awards as the Conference matured. Craftspeople using the different elements in their work qualify for consideration based upon originality, craftsmanship and to the degree that the element has been used in their work.

Best Artist *Leather*

2000
Cowgirl's Choice
Yocham's Custom Leather
Rick & Rhonda Yocham
Bartlesville, Oklahoma

1999
Woodland Armoire
Chapman Designs
Chris Chapman
Carbondale, Colorado

1998
Ladies Astride Saddle
Southfork Saddlery
Verlane Desgrange
Cody, Wyoming

1997
Roper II
Chapman Designs
Chris Chapman
Carbondale, Colorado

2001
My Ancestors Would Be Proud
18th Century Scottish Chest
Chapman Designs
Chris Chapman
Carbondale, Colorado

Best Artist *Fashion & Jewelry*

2001

Day Four, Rendezvous Royale
Anne Beard
Lexington, Oregon
Photo: David Wesley Vaughan

2000

Elk River Treasure
Elk River Beadworks
Suzanne M.M. Warner
Joliet, Montana

1999

Flight of the Nez Perce in 1877
Hitching Tails
Ron & Shoni Maulding
Kettle Falls, Washington

1998

Landscape Bolo Tie
SISU Designs
Thomas Beaman
Black Mountain, North Carolina

1997

Purple Sage Smoking Jacket
Anne Beard
Lexington, Oregon

Best Artist Accents

2001

Forest Spirit Ceiling Light
Dancing Light Lamps
Cloudbird
Twisp, Washington

Photo: Elijah Cobb

Best *Collection*

This award was created in 1999 to honor the designer who has created a collection with a common design theme and is consistent in fabric, embellishment and overall appearance.

2001
Women of the Wild West
Pate Stetson
Big Timber, Montana
Photo: David Wesley Vaughan

2000
The Silver Spur Collection
Suze Wood
Seattle, Washington

1999
Magpie Designs
Karen Bonnie
Abiquiu, New Mexico

Best *Adaptation* of Materials

In 1999, this Award was created for the designer who demonstrates a particularly creative use of traditional materials.

2001

Alan Michael USA Leatherworks
Alan Michael
Beverly Hills, California
Photo: David Wesley Vaughan

2000

Hilary Smith Company
Hilary Smith
Taos, New Mexico

1999

Wyoming Custom Leather
Randy Krier
Cody, Wyoming

2001

Tried and True
Quandary Design
Leadville, CO
Photo: Buffalo Bill Historical Center

Switchback Ranch
Purchase Award

This Award is given through the generosity of Buffalo Bill Historical Center Patron David Leuschen and allows the Buffalo Bill Historical Center to purchase a piece or pieces to place in its permanent collection of Western Decorative Arts. Some of the pieces are currently on display in the Cody Style exhibit.

2000
Teton Settee
Norseman Designs West
John Gallis
Cody, Wyoming

1999
Sky King Table
Mark Koons
Wheatland, Wyoming

1998
Cowhide & Tooled Leather Fainting Couch
Yocham's Custom Leather
Rick & Rhonda Yocham
Bartlesville, Oklahoma

1998
Anti-Gravity Table
New West
J. Mike Patrick
Cody, Wyoming

1997
Hallway Table
Quandary Designs
Leadville, Colorado

1997
Rocky Mountain Ceiling Lamp
Cash Metals
John & Kerry Cash
Cody, Wyoming

1997
Purple Sage Smoking Jacket
Anne Beard
Lexington, Oregon

1996
The Art Shoppe
Bozeman, Montana

1996
Cavalry & Indians
Triangle Z Ranch Furniture
Kendall Siggins
Cody, Wyoming

1995
Buffet
Red Bird Furniture
Rocky & Tawnya Wilson
Dubois, Wyoming

1995
The Bronze Moose Panel Lamp With Rawhide Shade
The Rainbow Trail Collection
John & Pam Mortensen
Wilson, Wyoming

1994
Corral Creek Sideboard
Covert Workshops
Jim & Lynda Covert
Cody, Wyoming
Carving done by Ron Skenandore

Best Western *Spirit*

Established in 1997, this award is given to the piece that represents exceptional creativity in expressing the Spirit of the West.

2001
Copper Creek Camper
Montana Wagons
Hilary Heminway & Terry Baird
McLeod, Montana
Photo: Audrey Hall

2000
Outlaw Cabinet
Greenwood Designs
Brad & Lorraine Greenwood
Clio, California

1999
Spirits Untamed
Amber Jean
Livingston, Montana

in collaboration with

High Country Designs
Don & Steve Butts
Frisco, Colorado

1998
Outhouse
Montana Wagons
Hilary Heminway & Terry Baird
McLeod, Montana

1998
Cowgirl Cameo Ottoman
Anne Beard
Lexington, Oregon

1997
The Wild Bench
Thom Ross & Tim Groth
Boise, Idaho

1997
Neon Dream
Pat Olson Sculpture
& Furniture Art
Pat Olson
Grand Junction, Colorado

Martin Harris Award of Excellence

Established by Marty Kruzich and Jan Lindsay to provide recognition to craftspeople who go the extra mile to perfect craftsmanship and bring extraordinary designs to the exhibition floor of the Western Design Conference.

2001
The Yellowstone Desk
Norseman Designs West
John Gallis
Cody, WY
Photo: Elijah Cobb

2000
Pony Express Desk III & Switchback Chair
Norseman Designs West
John Gallis
Cody, Wyoming

1999
Woodland Armoire
Chapman Designs
Chris Chapman
Carbondale, Colorado

The Cody Award for Western Design recognizes an individual or entity for outstanding achievement in the field. It is given by the Western Design Institute Board of Directors in cooperation with the Buffalo Bill Historical Center.

2000 Manuel
Nashville, Tennessee

Manuel – the man whose clothes Vogue calls "Cowboy Couture" and who Rolling Stone says is "the couturier of Rock 'n Roll". He's the man who put Elvis in a jumpsuit and made Johnny Cash "the Man in Black".

1999 Ruth Taggart Blair
Cody, Wyoming

Her illustrious career included five years at W & J Sloane in San Francisco as a designer. Later, she worked closely with Thomas Molesworth. The furnishings and custom designs of the TE Ranch being the highlight of her Molesworth years.

1998 Yellowstone National Park

Yellowstone National Park was honored for their commitment to fine craft and design in the restoration of key architectural elements within the Park.

1995 Gibbs Smith, Publisher
Layton, Utah.

Gibbs' publications have generated enthusiasm for western design and continues to enlighten and entertain lovers of the West.

1994 Lonn Taylor, Historian,
National Museum of American History
Smithsonian Institution, Washington, D.C.

Mr. Taylor is the author of several books and numerous articles on the decorative arts and architecture in the American Southwest.

Additional Awards

In the early years, the possibility of receiving an award at the Western Design Conference was not the impetus for participation. Certainly there was a sense of satisfaction at being the "best" in one's class but the ultimate reward was the value of the "gathering"itself - contacts were made, ideas were exchanged and ultimately participants left with much more than they came with – a resurgence of enthusiasm for their craft. If a ribbon and $25 was also in their pocket, then the ride home was that much sweeter.

It was this same spirit of camaraderie, which prompted the one-time award presented to Gary Phillips in 1993. A vehicle mishap while enroute to the Conference took his piece out of the running for "Best of" anything. Gary, however, was not to go home empty-handed – a tribute to his perseverance for "patching it together" and getting to the show - Gary was presented with the first "Hard Luck Award." Let's hope it's the last.

From 1993-95, the Conference was conducted in a trade show format and as such, "Best Exhibit" was a natural point of recognition. As the Conference has evolved into a "gallery" format, this particular award is no longer in use. Things do have a way of coming full circle...so don't count it out for good.

From inception, the Conference has awarded craftspeople and designers for their outstanding quality of workmanship. In recent years, however, the scope and class of awards has increased significantly due largely to the generous contributions of private individuals and institutions.

1993 Best Exhibit

Triangle Z Ranch Furniture
Kendall Siggins
Cody, Wyoming

1994 Best Exhibit

New West
J. Mike Patrick
Cody, Wyoming

1995 Best Exhibit

Montana Cottonwood

1993 Hard Luck

Gary Phillips
The Drawknife

1996 Most Creative Use of Materials

MacPhail's Studio
Dan MacPhail
Kevil, Kentucky

Art Accents Accessories

44

Detail: David LaMure Jr. Studios
David LaMure
Kimberly, Idaho

Accenting the West

by *Chase Reynolds Ewald*

The West has always represented unlimited opportunity. It's a place where there's freedom to experiment, to be your own person, to set your own style. This concept is vividly illustrated in Western decor. In other settings — whether a seaside cottage, a suburban Colonial, or an urban manse — rooms are accessorized with the expected: curtains, pillows, rugs, lamps, fine art. Step your cowboy-booted feet over the threshold of a log cabin, an adobe ranch house, or a restored barn, however, and you'll see Western variations on the same curtains, pillows, rugs, lamps, and fine art — as well as animal hides, antler art, lamps made from sculpture, cowboy boots used as bookends, vintage rodeo posters, Native American regalia, rustic antiques, old enamelware coffee pots, collections of Western salt-and-pepper shakers or Indian arrowheads, vintage bits and spurs, fishing rods, and saddles. There might even be a canoe hanging from the rafters, or a wagon wheel leaning against the wall.

Explains interior designer Hilary Heminway, "Ranchers saw these wagon wheels outside. Every day they were working with them. Rather than just letting them rot outside, they brought them in. It's part of that Western urge to recycle, to make do. They'd say, 'Let's see how we can make it useful.' "

Breathing new life into an item that has outlived its original use is a strong tendency for Western designers. The wagon wheel whose wood is too dried up and cracked to bear the weight of a carriage can

Come Dancers, Spotted Horse Studios
A.D. Tonnessen, Austin, Texas

45

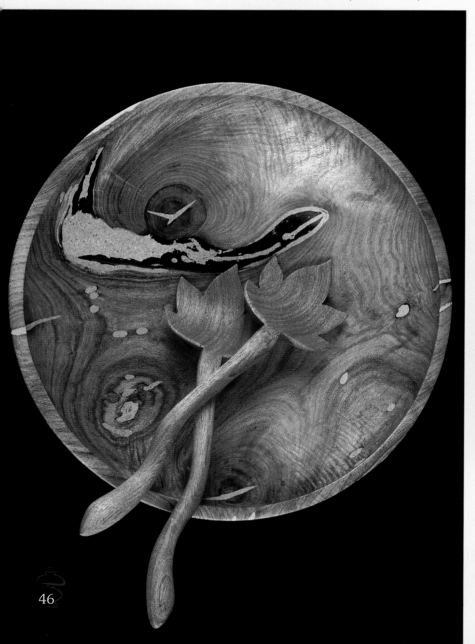

Salad Set, Treestump Woodcrafts
Ron and Christine Sisco, Tumacacori, Arizona

support a glass tabletop or mark the entrance to a driveway; the coffee grinder that no longer grinds is just the right size for a lamp base. Worn down horseshoes can be bent into handles or hat racks, or welded together to form a bootjack. Even guns become decorative when stored in a (locked, of course) cabinet.

Similarly, in a Western setting, items that would usually be strictly functional are often created as art, whether it's a metal pot rack cut out with silhouettes of wildlife, a wrought-iron fireplace screen depicting the surrounding mountains, or a museum-quality bronze sculpture crafted as a lamp. In the hands of a skilled and committed craftsperson, these resources become fine works of art in their own right. Perhaps westerners, who in the early days kept so few possessions, are inherently open to the idea that just because it's functional doesn't mean it's not beautiful. "A saddle is a saddle," says Hilary Heminway. "There are plain-looking saddles and there are ones that have been accessorized. People ride both." But those with eloquent designs are also invited into the living room. "Just because you don't hang it on the wall," she adds, "doesn't mean it's not art."

The overriding influence of the West's landscape and lifestyle certainly follows people indoors as well. An antler found nestled in the grass among the sagebrush is a treasure with so many uses: as candlestick, as hat rack, as drawer pull, as a backdrop to scrimshaw-like artwork. Intriguingly shaped branches might become a candelabra or a sconce, while straight twigs can be woven together as placemats. An elk hide can be thrown on the floor, hung on the wall, or decorated with strips of beadwork and made into pillows. As one Western craftsman puts it, Western artisans are limited only by their imagination.

Byron Price is the Director of the Charles M. Russell Center for the Study of Art in the American West at the University of Oklahoma. He suggests that, even given the often humble materials, it's just a fine line that divides Western craftsmanship from art. And, he adds, "By broadening people's ideas of Western art, you're giving them a better opportunity to understand Western art in general."

The work — whether it's painting on hides or carving leather or weaving beads or firing a design into pottery or hooking wool into a rug — is simply artistry applied to an unusual canvas. "In some ways, art in the traditional sense is getting a new life in another venue," says

Santa Fe Chandelier
Cash Metals, John and Kerry Cash
Cody, Wyoming

Price. "For instance, a saddle with artistic scenes in leather: when they began doing it they were imitating Charlie Russell paintings, then they branched out. But craftspeople have to consider the same artistic elements — balance, texture, composition — whether they're designing furniture or bits and spurs.

"Artists are driven to create, whether they have the luxury of paints and canvas or must rely on the materials at hand. It's no wonder that the West — with its dramatic vistas and yearly cycle of short bursts of outdoor activity followed by months of indoor creative time — inspires such a broad array of uniquely expressive artistry. But, while characteristic of the region, it is not unprecedented," says Byron Price.

"Western arts and crafts are the extension of a long tradition that has a Western manifestation but has been around a long time," he says. "My research shows that Western horsehair braiding goes way back. People in Russia and the Ukraine were producing items in the 17th, 16th, and 15th Centuries that looked like they were made at Deer Lodge Prison, things like quirts and watch chains. The color schemes and patterns bear a striking resemblance to things that were produced in the nineteenth century American West. It lies in the connection of all horse cultures. But I've always said Western art as a phenomenon is not created in a vacuum, immune from outside influence. It's very diverse, and one has to expect a lot of intended and unintended influence. And it's not just in a slavish interpretation, not just in trying to replicate what came from the East or Mexico, but it is infused with the West itself."

What makes each piece unique and of the moment, Price says, is "the craftsperson's relationship to the land, and the atmosphere the person finds himself in." That's how Western interiors can be so individually expressive — while still remaining so quintessentially Western.

John & Kerry Cash

Cash Metals

Established in 1990, Cash Metals is family owned and operated. John, a native of Cody, has been welding for 23 years; Kerry, who grew up in Montana, has a background in art and design. Together, they've produced a line of wall sconces, chandeliers, switch plates, table lamps, towel bars and rings, furniture, floor lamps, firescreens, mirrors, coat racks and photo frames; their products are handcrafted of iron, with rawhide, mica, wood and glass and they particularly enjoy one-of-a-kind commissions. Cash Metals' designs are based on western heritage and native mountain wildlife. Their Rocky Mountain chandelier features pine trees, moose, elk and deer against a background of mountains; the Longhorn Vanity incorporates the horns of a longhorn bull in a tableau of cowboys relaxing around a campfire under a crescent moon. Their newest creation, a series of mini hanging lights in the form of sagebrush and tumbleweeds, was inspired by "the naturally unique shapes of sagebrush and tumbleweeds prevalent in Wyoming."

Photo: Mack Frost

Larry Glaze

Antler Art of the Plains

Larry Glaze considers himself an "environmental artist." He gets all his ideas straight from nature, from the wild deer and turkeys that mingle with the horses on his property, and the materials that are found on his Missouri farm. The wood for his sculpture and lamp bases, for instance, comes from wind-downed Osage orange trees native to the region. "It's a very hard wood," he explains. "And it's a beautiful wood, yellow in color and hard like iron." The antlers he uses for his eagle sculptures, chandeliers, and lamps are all naturally shed; he uses moose antlers from Alaska, elk from the Rockies, and whitetail deer from the forest on his farm and the surrounding Ozark Hills. A self-trained artist, Glaze's Cherokee heritage is reflected in his environmental ethic and his subject matter. His most notable work, an American eagle fashioned from moose antlers with a bronze-patina head and feathers on an Osage orange tree trunk base, has been commissioned by organizations, businesses, and individuals, including the President of the United States.

Photo: Elijah Cobb

49

Glenn F. Gilmore

Gilmore Metalsmithing Studio

Glenn Gilmore has won international awards for his hand-wrought furniture, fireplace screens, andirons, sconces, and gates depicting elk, the mountains, oak leaves and acorns and crabs among the beach grasses. Gilmore cites a range of influences in his artistic life: "Life experiences, nature, the mountains of the West, road trips, parents and family, and Frank Turley," founder of the Turley School of Blacksmithing in Santa Fe. A graduate of the Wolverine Farriers School in Michigan, Gilmore embarked on architectural blacksmithing in the early 1980's; he studied metal design in Germany, forged metalwork in European museums, and worked at a forge in Aachen, Germany. Gilmore works with ferrous and non-ferrous metals using hot and cold forging techniques and traditional joinery. "I enjoy using bold clean lines in my designs, always striving for a balance between mass, form and function. I want the piece to have enough body that it will stand on its own, yet not be lost or feel overwhelming." Since the early '80's, Gilmore's work has been represented in juried and invitational shows, in galleries and museums throughout the United States. Glenn shares his skills at workshops and seminars in Germany and the United States.

Photo: McNabb Studio

50

Robert Morris

Grand Illusions

In the world of Robert Morris, things are not always what they seem. A whitewashed log headboard, with its knotholes, irregular shapes, and bowed top rail, is actually a flat piece of plywood, cut, shaped, and painted in the "trompe l'oeil" style. Morris' work does indeed "trick the eye," whether it's cowboy furniture, oversized wooden chargers painted to look like leather with whipstitched edging, or the large murals he's commissioned to paint in restaurants and other interiors around the country. A resident of Sonoma Valley, a quieter, more western part of the California wine country distinguished by its historic Spanish Mission, Morris studied art at The Art Center School of Design in Pasadena, California, then went on to design cowboy motifs for a chain of restaurants, build Western-themed furniture, and, for eighteen years, make teeth for celebrities. A fine-art painter and photographer who works out of a rural barn studio, Morris has about half completed his major opus, a collection of more than 300 paintings of contemporary Native Americans, each representing a different tribe. His ultimate goal is to find a philanthropic buyer for "The Last Americans" who will donate the collection to a Western museum. "My life is my work," he says. "My work is my life."

51

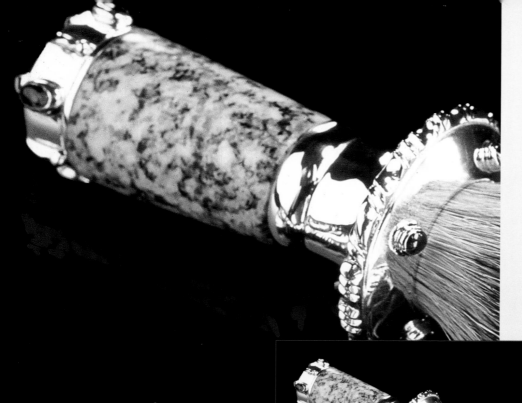

Jim &
Maggi
Dunakin

Dunakin Design

Jim Dunakin has been making jewelry for thirty years; Jim and Maggi Dunakin have been making jewelry together for the past five years. Today, the photo journal that chronicles their work holds images of 4300 one-of-a-kind pieces. The Dunakins' sculpture and jewelry are made from sterling silver and/or gold, with stone and occasional accents of copper and brass. Sometimes Jim incorporates bone, glass, horn, and other found materials he picks up on his daily hikes, and he favors 10,000-year-old fossil ivory, mined from Alaskan glaciers by natives of that region. Maggi works the stones — cutting, grinding, and polishing — then Jim designs the jewelry around the finished stones, doing all the metalwork by hand. Jim Dunakin's style is unique, and immediately recognizable. He loves big-city architecture and American freeway culture, yet, "whenever I leave, I long for my quiet life in the mountains of Montana. My work is a reflection of this dichotomy, a juxtaposition of extremes: faceted precious stones with bones and river pebbles; tortured, twisted, and scorched metals against the lovingly polished."

Photo: David Egan

Kirk Rexroat

Rexroat Knives

Born and raised in Wyoming, Kirk Rexroat was first inspired by his outdoor lifestyle to try his hand at knife-making some twenty years ago. Since then he has attained the status of mastersmith in the American Bladesmith Association and won numerous awards and honors. Today, his knives are more likely to be kept in a display case than to be used on elk hunts. "By studying books filled with photos of antique knives, I gain a feeling for certain eras and geography in relation to styles. These images influence my designs, as do my purchases of presentation woods from around the world: mastadon ivory from the frozen tundra of Alaska or Russia, or pearl from the depths of the ocean. These influences often inspire my knives to take on a theme, such as one whose Damascus blade pattern was reminiscent of duck feathers; its bolsters were engraved with cattails and mallard ducks were scrimshawed in the ancient ivory." A bowie knife, a symbol of the West, captures Wyoming's bucking horse in mosaic Damascus down its blade. Rexroat's favorite process, he says, "is the creating of Damascus, the process of layering different metals, manipulating and forge-welding them together to create various patterns in the blade. With each blow of the hammer and ring of the anvil, my ideas take shape."

Photo: Holly Rexroat

Tony Alvis

Wilderness Iron Works

Tony Alvis comes from a long line of blacksmiths and lives amidst the splendid scenery of coastal California while immersed in vestiges of the area's rich Spanish Californian past. His workshop is located at an old feedlot across from the Ventura Mission at the foot of the Los Padres Mountains. From there, says the artisan, "You can see the islands shining on the water" of the Santa Barbara Channel. In the nearby mountains, where Alvis pulls a pack string as a commercial outfitter, roam elk, deer, black bear and condors. A self-taught artist and master blacksmith with a background in ornamental ironwork, Alvis conceived of his first piece while contemplating his own silhouette, and that of his horse and the string of packed mules behind him. The one time horseshoer is now known nationally for the meticulous detail in his fireplace screens, lighting fixtures, and still lifes. As a child growing up in Pasadena, he was influenced by the Arts & Crafts Movement and Native American art of the Southwest; later, he studied the art of Charlie Russell, Frederic Remington, and Jo Mora. These influences blend seamlessly in his work. Starting with sheets of steel, he explains, "You just work it. I pound the hell out of it. It's hard on the body, but I want to give it a real textured look so it looks old. A lot of people think my pieces are old. Most of this type of work is generic-looking or plain," he adds. "When I cut out, you can see the light shining through and the muscle tone on the cowboys."

Photo: Scott Star

Cloudbird

Dancing Light Lamps

Cloudbird's defining life experience was her time in the Alaskan bush, where she spent eleven years living the life of a hunter-gatherer. There she observed "the balance and timing of nature, the asymmetry yet utter perfection of beauty. Through total immersion in a spectacular but often dangerous environment, I learned attunement. At a time when America was becoming fast-track, I was wholly dependent on my skills of observation and insight, discipline and completion." This intimacy with nature reveals itself in her leather, rawhide, and beadwork — which she combines with hand-forged metalwork — to create unique lamps. "I work with several highly qualified blacksmiths. Their shops turn out exceptional hand-forged items. They work with my design specifications, with room to find their own hand in the process." Cloudbird has worked with leather, making moccasins, mittens, hats, and garments, for twenty years, but lamps are her favorite vehicle of expression. Of the meticulous handwork required in Cloudbird's beading and leatherwork, she says, "I consider my work a meditation — long hours of aloneness but each step in an often tedious process builds toward that inner vision of one thing that is not just a thing but an item cherished."

Photo: R. L. I. Photography

55

Supaya
Gray Wolfe

Many Tears

Born in the Cherokee Nation, Supaya Gray Wolfe has spent the last twenty years on the Navajo Reservation, where she lives in a hogan, the traditional Navajo dwelling; she spends the summer months in a mountain cabin near Durango, Colorado. Both settings have informed her work. "I did not find much interesting in a classroom but there's a lot to learn in a hogan, a kiva, or at a Sundance." Spending time with the elders at Pine Ridge, South Dakota, and learning from her Navajo "heart mother" — hearing the old stories and seeing antique clothing — has been a big inspiration to her as well. Gray Wolfe works in buffalo hides, which she gets from a friend who ranches buffalo for meat. "I meet the buffalo before they die. I feed them, spend time with them. And this way, when I work with their hides, I know them." Gray Wolfe makes reproduction Native American clothing and accoutrements from the 1800's to the early 1900's, using beadwork, fringe, feathers, and other traditional materials. "It brings much joy to me to do my work and deliver it to the homes of people who take really good care of it. I go away knowing my pieces will be around for their grandchildren to enjoy. That's what it's all about, to teach the children."

Photo: E. L. Abrahamson Jr.

56

Vicki Cudney

Quality Hitched Horsehair

Vicki Cudney learned the fine art of horsehair hitching from "a guy from the Deer Lodge Prison," an institution famous for its mastery of the old-time craft of horsehair hitching (its inhabitants were among the few people willing to give the craft the time it required). A native of Colorado and a resident of Montana for the past twenty-five years, Cudney works in hunting camps and helps with night calving on cattle ranches; she also spends a lot of time at horse-related events. "I like working mostly with natural colors and I find making horse gear — old-style bridles, quirts, and hobbles — to be the most interesting." Connoisseurs certainly find her work compelling; it has been featured in books and selected for many prestigious shows including the *Cowboy Poetry Gathering* in Elko, Nevada, and the *Trappings of the American West* show in Flagstaff.

Photo: Wendy Deans

57

Rik Mettes
&
Brenda Bales

Heart Mountain Forge & Design

Rik Mettes started working with metal as a blacksmith almost thirty years ago. He later studied ornamental and architectural works, ultimately developing his own line of functional art. His fire tools, gates, weather vanes, wine racks, chandeliers, and furniture are hand-crafted using old-world methods, such as traditional joinery. Brenda Bales has been working with Mettes for the past four years. "Although we work in a number of metals, iron is our favorite as it is one of the strongest, toughest, and most versatile elements. Iron can be forged into any form imaginable—either massive or delicate." Over the years they've developed their own style, such as a table combining wood and iron. "While on our way to explore some of the many caves in the Big Horn Mountains, we found ourselves admiring stands of fire-kill cedar trees for their almost outrageous craggy beauty. A week later, we returned to harvest a number of these intriguing specimens. We then used a particularly interesting section of one tree as the transitional focal point of this piece, in between a more traditional iron top and a contemporary iron interpretation as the base." Heart Mountain's designs, say Mettes and Bales, "are a combination of old-world methods and contemporary creativity."

58

Photo: Kathleen Hayden

Tim Preston

Preston Pottery

Tim Preston has been working with clay for twenty-eight years; he studied art at two different colleges, and currently teaches pottery classes. His pieces made with horsehair are distinctive vessels whose burnt lines in earth tones suggest the landscapes of his native Colorado. "I was born and raised in Colorado and have always felt a connection to the natural beauty of the Rocky Mountains and the eastern plains of Colorado." Preston's vessels are thrown on a potter's wheel, burnished to achieve a glass-like finish, then fired in a kiln and removed at about 1000 degrees. "My wife, Debbie, creates the designs with horsehair generously provided by our horse, Spike. The process has been described by friends as the Horse Hair Dance; Debbie circles around me as I slowly rotate the pot, placing the hair carefully so as not to burn herself. The hair ignites on contact, creating the black lines and plumes of smoke across the clay, but we have to move quickly because as the pot cools, the hair will no longer leave a mark." Although for years Preston created more functional pieces, such as casseroles and teapots, "I find my work evolving into more decorative, one-of-a-kind pieces that are valued for their visual appearance more than for their function."

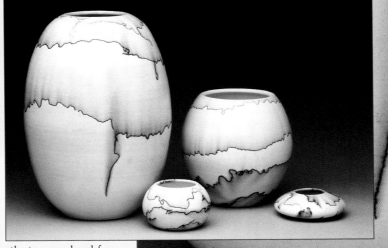

Photo: Ted Chavez

59

Jeremy, Chris
&
Andrew George

Frontier Ironworks

Jeremy, Chris and Andrew George grew up in Oklahoma and Texas working on land development projects, and they learned construction and welding techniques early. Their hobby — building metal furniture and lighting — became their fulltime business six years ago. Now, Frontier Ironworks offers three distinct lines to wholesalers throughout the western United States and Canada. The *Western* line features cowboy and ranch imagery, the *Wilderness* line celebrates mountain scenery and wildlife, and the *Country and Southwest* line employs images from nature, such as pinecones and Native American design motifs. The brothers welcome custom work and enjoy developing one-of-a-kind pieces. One of their most ambitious projects was their *Migration Chandelier*, featuring a giant rawhide teepee in the midst of a mountain scene, with a bull and cow elk migrating around the mountain. Frontier Iron works, says Andrew, "started as an idea with very little know-how but with the support of friends and family grew into an occupation that enables each of us to express our strengths. Since then we have always seen it as an asset to encourage the Western way of life and to preserve our heritage."

William M. Davis

Northern Lights

A fine artist for the past thirty years, Bill Davis combines art and function in his cast-bronze lamps and lighting fixtures. Widely renowned for the exquisite detail in his sculptures and also an accomplished water-color painter, Davis' works reside in many private and museum collections. In recent years, says the artist, "I have become an advocate of art having function." A Davis lamp might be formed from a bronze sculpture of a black bear and her cubs climbing a tree, and crowned with a Tiffany-style art-glass shade. A billiard table lamp incorporates bas-relief work in bronze of bison, horses and Plains Indian villages. "Yellowstone and the Absarokas are my inspiration; the hunting, fly fishing and outdoor pursuits of photography and birding have given my work authenticity not learned from books. Having horses and dogs has given me a familiarity with animal anatomy. Being an outdoor enthusiast and doing ranch-related hobbies — the love of these things is not only an educational experience but also the passion for these things carries over in my work."

Photo: Elijah Cobb

61

MKR Design, Inc.

A native of Finland, Marjatta Salvat grew up in a family of knitters, weavers and spinners of wool; she holds a BFA degree in Fiber Arts from the University of Wisconsin-Milwaukee. She has made wall hangings for corporate and private clients, designed costumes for a theatre company and worked as an artist-in-residence in Colorado schools. In 1996, Salvat discovered a unique hand-tufting technique and has been tufting rugs ever since. The one-of-a-kind rugs are designed and made by Salvat, using custom-dyed 100% wool. The designs are created to compliment the color scheme of each interior and the specific needs of the customer. Salvat also produces limited-edition rugs, in editions of thirty, which are hand-tufted by craftspeople in India. Salvat's designs are inspired by the landscapes and lifestyles of the West. As a child she grew up watching American television shows like Bonanza and Rawhide; she developed a love of nature through family hikes in the woods; "My father called it our Sunday church," she recalls. Her work still evokes her memories of Finland and the inspiration of the West: "The colors as they are in the midwinter in Finland are the colors of dust in the mountains and forests with a stripe of setting sun." Through her work she attempts to capture "the balance of it all."

Sonny Tuttle

Red Nations Art

Master craftsman Sonny Tuttle has been practicing his art for a full half-century; he's the founder of Red Nations Art, an organization of artists from the Sioux, Arapaho, Flathead, Yakima, Acoma, Laguna and Navajo nations which promotes museum-quality art in the style of the High Plains people. The group's specialty is hide paintings, which, Tuttle says, "express our traditions, our beliefs, our spiritual values, and our history." Born on the Pine Ridge Sioux Reservation, Tuttle has lived on the Wind River Indian Reservation for the past forty-five years, where the traditions of his Lakota heritage have informed his life. Many of Red Nations' artisans are active in religious ceremonies and are avid participants in Plains Indians powwows. "The old nomadic people expressed nearly all of their rich art in the cultural and religious objects that were used daily. Many of these items are as meaningful and useful today as they were in the days of the buffalo."

63

Leon Sanderson
&
Jill Judd

Sanderson Studio

Diverse in subject and large in scale, Leon Sanderson and Jill Judd's art, furniture, and accessories are handcrafted from native Wyoming woods such as white pine, Douglas fir, spruce, lodgepole pine and cottonwood. A custom-sculpted door might feature a full-sized grizzly bear, while a simple burl bowl lets the beauty of the wood serve as its own adornment. Furniture is painted or carved with wildlife, fly-fishing or nature imagery. Leon has appreciated the beauty and usefulness of wood since he was a child growing up in a timber-oriented community in Oregon. After stints in the military and at a lumber mill, Leon started a construction business; fifteen years later, he sold it to pursue his passion: wood sculpting. Jill — a lifelong artist working in painting, photography, graphic design and leather — joined Leon in establishing Sanderson Studio in 1991. Leon's wood-sculpting style is unique and he devotes much time to fine-sanding. Jill has developed a process for painting and glazing that enhances the grain and texture of the wood. "Sculpture is an unveiling process," says Leon. "I look for the heart and soul of the wood to reveal itself as my sculpture takes shape around it."

Photo: Jill Judd

Angie Nelson

Free Rein Studio

Originating in 14th-century France and later regarded as an economic alternative to carpet, floorcloths today offer a fresh change from area rugs. An "original painting for your floor," floorcloths are made from layers of primer, paint and sealer over heavy-weight canvas; they can withstand years of heavy use. Angie Nelson's designs — inspired by nature, horses, her North Carolina farm and the West — range from "Autumn Walk," a stone path scattered with autumn leaves, to "Art of the Sioux," with horses, a Plains Indian shield used as a central medallion and a Native American graphic motif. Recently she has experimented with visually textured canvases incorporating leather, sequins, beads and metal, and has made wall cloths, placemats and even some small furniture pieces. Nelson's grandmother "was creative out of necessity. She taught me that being resourceful made your creations special." Her father "shared his love of horses and all things cowboy. I was so 'not cool' in my boots and jeans at school in North Carolina, but I knew where my heart was and is today."

Photo: Lori Richey

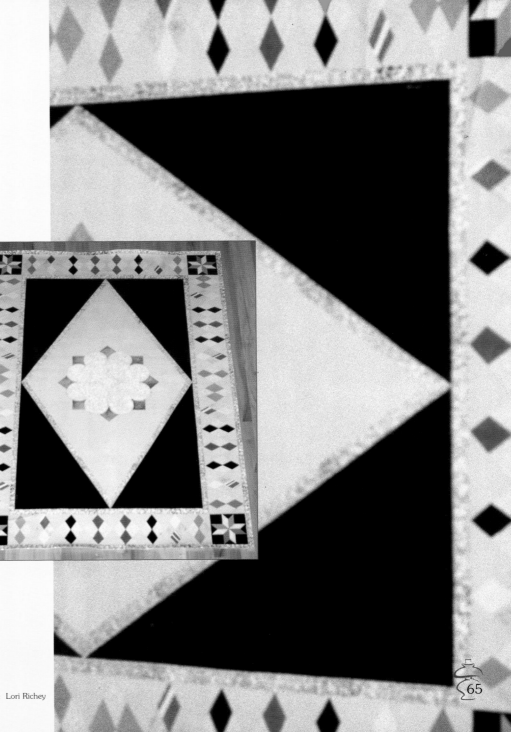

Bill Feeley

Art 'N' Iron

A lifetime resident of Cody, Wyoming, Bill Feeley has worked as a big-game guide for over thirty years, worked on a cattle ranch, and even tried his luck with the bucking horses. "I've seen the hurt and humor of the West," he says, "and I love portraying that in my art." Rather than employing generic images of whitetail deer grazing in a meadow, for instance, he shows two bucks startled by pheasants in flight. His wildflower chandelier hangs from hand-forged horseshoes and features a joyous profusion of accurately shaped and colored native Rocky Mountain wildflowers; the rawhide shade features handpainted shooting stars. Feeley began working in his father's concrete business at the age of fifteen, opened a welding shop in 1975 and started sculpting wildlife bronzes in 1979. "I welded by day and sculpted by night." In 1985, he began making iron home furnishings with Western and wildlife motifs. He now works on an old blacksmith forge, inherited from his grandfather, to design items with an old wrought-iron look.

66

Photo: Elijah Cobb

Patti Rooks

Bunkhouse Gallery

A native Texan, Patti Rooks practices her art – Scherenschnitte, or the art of paper cutting – at her kitchen table on a working ranch in Colorado. There she is moved to incorporate vestiges of her family's life into the imagery she applies to lampshades. "Where I live has probably the greatest influence on my cuttings and the ability to see ranch life from the inside has brought reality and functionality to my pieces." Craftsmanship flourishes in the Rooks household; Patti's husband is a bit-and-spur maker, her brother-in-law is a custom boot maker, and both her daughters also practice paper cutting. Rooks' craft has been enhanced in a collaboration with Arizona artist Dave Holl, whose designs she has incorporated in her lampshades to great effect. Rooks has been studying the art of paper cutting since 1982, when she discovered its rich history while collecting antique silhouettes. "In recent years I have evolved my work, expanding the traditional German art with new designs and themes and combining it with other crafts and art. It keeps it interesting for me, with more challenges to expand my boundaries and also introduces the uniqueness of the art to more people."

Photo: Grant Heilman

Cindy Bennett

Cindy Bennett
Art & Design

A professional artist with two art degrees and many exhibits and fellowships behind her, Cindy Bennett's work speaks strongly of the West she knew as a child. Although she has lived in Los Angeles for the past twelve years, she grew up in Cody. "Growing up in northern Wyoming is the greatest visual influence on my work. The vast beauty and freedom of the environment is perpetually inspiring." Her early work focused on abstract acrylic landscapes with paint she mixed herself from industrial pigments; later, she used the paint on handmade paper in landscape collages and portraits. She completed a series of western landscapes in graduate school and later worked with oil and wax on canvas and wood. Ultimately, Bennett began photographing, then transfer-printing the resulting photos onto canvas, wood, paper and finally duiponi for lampshades. She then enhances the imagery with paint, creating what she calls illuminated monoprints. The Bison Antler Ranch lampshade grew out of a day spent documenting the bison at the Antler Ranch outside Meeteetse, Wyoming. "My formal training in the art gives me the tools to translate ideas into functional objects," she says.

68

YOU ARE CORDIALLY INVITED TO ATTEND

A PREMIER WESTERN ART EVENT FOR THE BENEFIT OF THE BUFFALO BILL HISTORICAL CENTER, CODY, WYOMING

FRIDAY AND SATURDAY, SEPTEMBER 20 & 21, 2002

Duke Beardsley, *Williams Fork Cowboy*, mixed media, 30 x 48 inches. People's Choice Award, 2001 Buffalo Bill Art Show and Sale.

2002 PARTICIPANTS

Cyrus Afsary
Arthur Amiotte
Joe Arnold
Clyde Aspevig
Dix Baines
Gerald Balciar
Nikolo Balkanski
Ty Barhaug
Bob Barlow
Duke Beardsley
Toby Birr
Buckeye Blake
Joseph Bohler
Nelson Boren
Kenneth Bunn
Reid Christie
Michael Coleman
Bunny Connell
John DeMott

Robert Deurloo
Steve Devenyns
Joellyn Duesberry
VaLoy Eaton
L.D. Edgar
John Encinias
Loren Entz
Tony Eubanks
John Fawcett
T.J. Feeley
Deborah Copenhaver Fellows
Fred Fellows
Mel Fillerup

Peter M. Fillerup
John Giarrizzo, Jr.
Walt Gonske
Glenna Goodacre
Bruce Graham
R.V. Greeves
David Halbach
Stefan Halvorsen
Ann Hanson
Harold T. Holden
Donna Howell-Sickles
Ramon Kelley
T.D. Kelsey

Joffa Kerr
Steve Kestrel
Everett Raymond Kinstler
Steven Lang
Robin Laws
Mehl Lawson
T. Allen Lawson
Laurie J. Lee
Linda Lillegraven
Mimi Litschauer
Walter T. Matia
Deanna Matteson
William Matthews

Gordon McConnell
Dave McGary
Jim Morgan
Ned Mueller
Christopher J. Navarro
E. Denney NeVille
Ralph Oberg
Julie Oriet
Joel Ostlind
Geoff Parker
Carol Peek
Andrew Peters
Larry Pirnie

Howard Post
Daryl Poulin
M.C. Poulsen
Linda S. Raynolds
Kevin Red Star
Grant Redden
William F. Reese
Sheila Rieman
Charles Ringer
Bonita Roberts
Thom Ross
Jeffrey B. Rudolph
Sherry Salari Sander

Steve Schrepferman
Robert Seabeck
Tim Shinabarger
Gary Shoop
Brett James Smith
George D. Smith
Matt Smith
Dean St. Clair
Linda St. Clair
Pati Stajcar
Phil Starke
Craig Tennant
Sonya Terpening
D. Michael Thomas
Karen Vance
M.W. Skip Whitcomb
Jim Wilcox
H. Randol Williford
Kathy Wipfler
Wayne E. Wolfe

BUFFALO BILL
ART SHOW & SALE
Cody, Wyoming

See the art on line—www.buffalobillartshow.com

PART OF "RENDEZVOUS ROYALE" WEEK, A CELEBRATION OF THE ARTS IN CODY, WY • *www.rendezvousroyale.org*

e-mail: art@codychamber.org • 307.587.5002 • 836 Sheridan Avenue • Cody, WY 82414 • fax: 307.527.6228

Simpson Gallagher Gallery

T.D. Kelsey   *Horse Power*   9"w x 17"l x 12"h, ed. of 5

A Fine Art Gallery Featuring Some of America's Leading Representational Artists

Gordon Allen, Clyde Aspevig, Dave Ballew, Bob Barlow, Toby Birr, Tina Close, Jimmy Dyer, Loren Entz, Carol Guzman, Tony Hochstetler, Harry Jackson

T.D. Kelsey, Steve Kestrel, Ron Kingswood, T. Allen Lawson, Bob Lemler, Kent Lemon, Mimi Litschauer, Michael J. Lynch, Walter Matia

William Matthews, Jim Morgan, Caroline Norton, Ralph Oberg, Joel Ostlind, Geoff Parker, Grant Redden, William F. Reese, Dan Robinson, Matt Smith

Margery Torrey, Skip Whitcomb, Hollis Williford, Kathy Wipfler, Ann Herzog Wright and Dan Young

1161 Sheridan Avenue • Cody, Wyoming 82414 • 307.587.4022 • sgallery@wavecom.net • www.sggfineart.com

COWBOY ORIGINALS BY

Russ Magowan

OLD WEST SIGNS ★ A FEW COWBOY BEDS ★ WESTERN SURPRISES

www.cowboybeds.com

ATLANTA, GEORGIA

Wilderness West Bronze

*F*unctional art sculpture with reflections of nature — fish and wildlife bronzes in exquisite tables and lamps, and bas-relief sculptures for hanging on walls. Bring the outdoors "in" — accent your home, lodge, cabin or office with functional western art.

wildernesswestbronze.com

Pat Love   drlove@intrq.net
208 Overland Trail

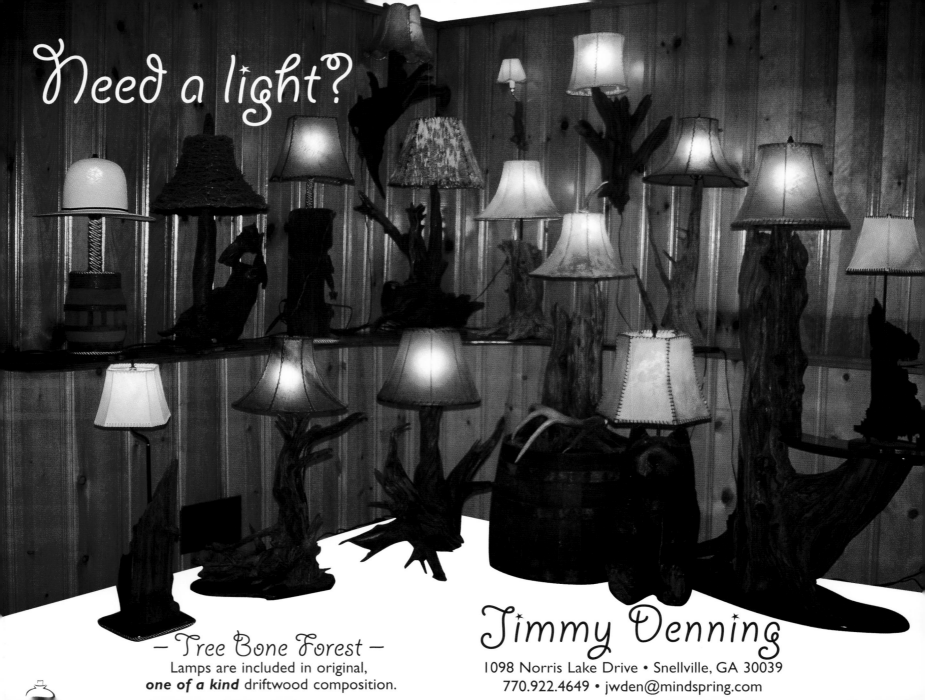

75

Art for the Hearth

Add the
finishing
touch to
your home
with custom
forged gates,
firescreens,
door hardware
and furniture.

Spirits in the Wind
Gallery

Fine Collection of Art by Nationally Acclaimed Artists

featuring

TY BARHAUG	JODY HORVATH	MARGO PETTERSON
KAREN BONNIE	GREG KELSEY	WALTER PIEHL
BOB BOOMER	JACK KOONCE	AMY POOR
DAVID CARICATO	DAVE LAMURE	JEFF RUDOLPH
L. D. EDGAR	JERRY MCKELLAR	RANDY VAN BEEK
SUSAN GUY	J. NELSON	LARRY VEEDER
MICHAEL HAMBY	JULIE ORIET	DAN YOUNG
K. HENDERSON	NEIL PATTERSON	SUPAYA GRAY WOLF

Spirits in the Wind Gallery

1211 Washington Ave., Golden CO 80401 • 303-279-1192 or 877-844-1609
www.spiritsinthewindgallery.com

78

CS Designs

TAOS VALLEY

Traditional and contemporary art
for home and office since 1992

Charlotte Shroyer

Taos, New Mexico
Genoa, Nevada

Personalized art services

Home and office art assessment

Art acquisition

Framing

Installation

CS Designs

Toll free 866.751.0375
New Mexico 505.751.0375
Nevada 775.782.7326

www.csdesignsco.com

Paula Schoen "Light of Love" oil on canvas. Horizon Fine Arts

Dave McGary "Short Bull" bronze. Horizon Fine Arts

Handcrafted jewelry. Leo Weaver Gallery

Handwoven pillows, Charlotte Shroyer

79

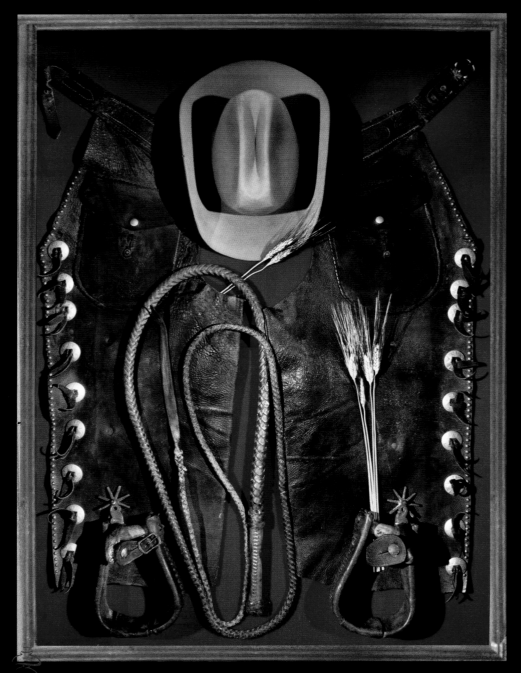

Old West Collection ™
Peter Hess
26500 Agoura Rd. Suite 591
Calabasas, CA 91302
Toll Free (866) 735 -4272
WWW.OldWestCollection.com

Peter Hess grew up in Calgary Alberta Canada, boasting the largest annual rodeo in the world, the Calgary Stampede. His fascination with Cowboys and Indians started at an early age, collecting western artifacts and relics for nearly 30 years. He moved to California in the early 1970s, utilizing his historical knowledge of the old west with respect to set design and prop coordination now observed in numerous western movies. His vastly traveled path nurtured his passion to explore many historical locations dating back to the old frontier. Continuing to collect vintage western rarities through the years, he now offers a remarkably unique and rare collection of western antiques. Inspired by the Native American culture and the era of the old west, he exhibits his artifacts in a unique art form, by encasing them in ornamental shadow boxes. This ensures their preservation and compliments any western décor with an original and authentic aesthetic presentation. The featured piece shown here is titled "The Last Roundup".This distinctive design exhibits turn of the century chaparrals, spurs, rawhide whip, stirrups & the classic Stetson hat. It is presently on loan to the Gene Autry Museum of Western Heritage. Many of Peter's works of art and antiques adorn the retreats of famous film stars and avid old west collectors. His entire collection can be viewed and artifacts purchased through the Old West Collection web site. In addition, he annually publishes a catalog in the form of a "coffee table" book that depicts all the old west collectibles that can be acquired. Those whom desire to commission Peter to design and create custom shadow boxes or original display cases for a client's own artifacts, may contact him at his studio workshop. For a personal consultation call toll free (866) RELICS2 or visit the website

@ www.oldwestcollection.com

VINTAGE COWBOY & INDIAN RARITIES

G.H. Leather Company

Houston, Texas
713-670-9800

*Keeping American
Indian Crafting
Skills Alive...*

INDIAN TERRITORY

of Cody Wyoming

1212 Sheridan Avenue
P.O. Box 1928
Cody, WY 82414
Phone (307) 527-5584
Fax (307) 527-5587
indianterritorycody.com

Wholesale ~ Retail

War Bonnet by Jeff Bluewater

85

GALLINGER TRAUNER DESIGNS, INC.
3490 Clubhouse Drive, Suite 101 • Wilson, WY 83014 • (307) 733-0902
at Teton Pines in Jackson Hole, Wyoming

DIANA BEATTIE INTERIORS

Designing Rustic Retreats in the Western Tradition

BIG HORN GALLERIES

NELSON BOREN

Nelson Boren "Lost Horse - Study" WC, 16"h x 12"w

DONNA HOWELL-SICKLES

Donna Howell-Sickles "Dog Kisses" Mixed Media , 60"h x 40"w

**The Big Horn Galleries salutes gallery artists participating in the Buffalo Bill Art Show.
Reception Saturday, Sept. 21st, 1-4 p.m.**

Significant Western Art

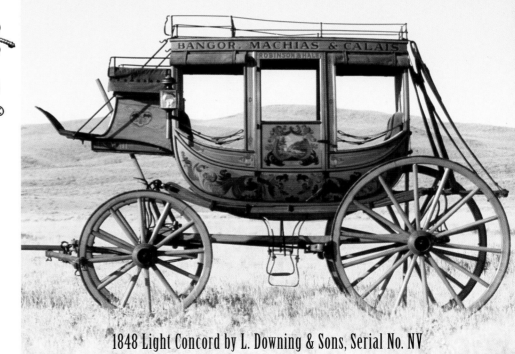

Fashion

Detail: Angela DeMontigny
Spirit Ware
Hagersville, Ontario

Wearing the West

by Chase Reynolds Ewald

Western fashion has always spanned a broad spectrum, from the colorful hues of the Spanish-Mexican palette seen in the Southwest to the proper lace-up-boots-and-parasol outfits of the Victorian era to the graceful beadwork-enhanced leathers of the Plains Indians. The classic Western look, though, has actually been a melding of different styles, even today easily distinguished by region, occupation, and lifestyle. A Nevada buckaroo, for instance, has always held to his own distinctive variation of the cowboy outfit, quite different from that of, say, a rancher in the Dakotas. The Wild West Show trick rider wore an outfit far removed, stylistically speaking, from the clothes of working ranch women. The miner, the logger, the mountain man and trapper — each had his own costume, all quintessentially western.

Despite this, there's a certain look, a certain line, a certain palette, and a sustained use of distinctive materials, which today, 150 years after the settling of the frontier, immediately says *Western* the world over.

"If you look," says Juti Winchester, curator of the Buffalo Bill Museum in Cody, "there are certain classic lines which have continued from the Wild West Show days to now: the fit of the jeans, the length of leg, the tiny waist for both men and women, skirts with a nipped-in waist and lots of flow at the ankles. That's what we saw 100 years ago, and it's what we see today. In any fashion," she adds, "it's the line that makes it recognizable and classic."

Sorrell Custom Boots, Lisa Sorrell, Guthrie, Oklahoma

Western styles have certainly evolved over the years— for women performers, they've gone from Victorian riding habits to spilt riding skirts to bright spangly jumpsuits to jeans with chaps — but they still retain certain characteristics. Attention to detail, for instance, is evident in the earliest works and still highlighted in not just the couture works being made today but even the mass-produced wear like Wrangler jeans, Carhartt jackets, and Wahmaker frontier-look vests.

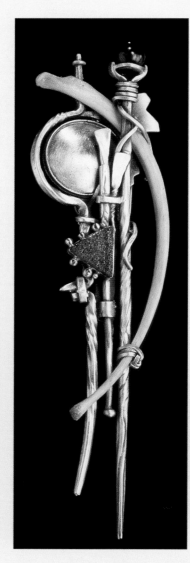

Lapis Dream
Dunakin Designs, Jim & Maggie Dunakin,
Big Timber, Montana

Early on, of course, all clothes were handmade and built to withstand the rigors of the frontier, from sturdy leathers sewn by mountain men to sensible woolens pieced together by pioneer women. Well before the appearance of glitz in rodeo arenas, style was important in a region populated by often itinerant people covering vast distances; their appearance had to speak for itself. Plains Indians spent hundreds of hours on intricate beadwork patterns for their garments, while others applied themselves to making beautiful, delicate patterns in carved leather and hitched horsehair, or braiding rawhide bridles, or insetting semi-precious stones into silver jewelry. Even the lowest paid cowboy kept a special pair of boots for going to town.

Over time, and with the influence of the Wild West shows at the turn of the century, rodeo's golden age in the 1920's and '30's, the Hollywood influence in the '40's and '50's, and the examples of Miss Rodeo America and professional rodeo competitors today, Western clothes became increasingly decorative, yet always remained highly functional.

"The clothes from the Golden Age were just beautiful," says Jennifer Nielsen, curator of the National Cowgirl Museum and Hall of Fame in Fort Worth, Texas. "A lot of the women were very good seamstresses. They had to be, because the clothes were getting beaten up all the time."

Eye-catching colors and details were born of necessity, Nielsen says. "They were designed so that people could see you in the arena, or so you'd look good on a black-and-white TV. They were designed to make an impact in an unforgiving medium." According to Art Emr, producer of a documentary on Roy Rogers and Dale Evans, Rogers began putting rhinestones on his costumes because he was concerned that the kids eight tiers up in Madison Square Garden couldn't see him.

In the history of Western fashion, says Juti Winchester, "I see a combination of romance and practicality." In a photo of cowgirls from a rodeo in the 1920's, "I see bloomers, split skirts, corduroy, embroidery, and fringe, but I also see soft blouses and flowy scarves and big hats. So while I'm galloping across the prairie, my scarf and my hair will be flowing in the wind."

Western fashion today pays homage to the past while looking forward to the future. Contemporary styles represent a wide array of references. A West Coast artist says she is inspired by the meeting and mixing of different cultures in the American West: Native Americans, European immigrants, Chinese laborers, and Spanish Mexicans. A California designer celebrates the icons she sees on western roadtrips: flowers, cactus, cowgirls, and horses. Spurs and rowels are recreated in a line of jewelry, while symbols of the Southwest like saguaro cactus adorn chenille coats. In the hands of a master craftsman, the humble cowboy boot — with remarkably intricate patterns of intertwined floral motifs, or a pattern of rainbow, moon, and stars — becomes a canvas for a rare art.

The enduring popularity of the Silver Screen era has created icons — both costumes and people — which are instantly recognizable. "They represented the spirit of the West and the romance of the West," says Art Emr, "and it was reflected in their clothes." Many people working in western fashion are still influenced by Hollywood's golden age. One designer describes her line as "Katherine Hepburn dressed by Dale Evans." Another chooses to evoke "the Western look of long ago." A third cites designs by Nudie as an important source of inspiration. Clearly, the Hollywood cowboy and the cowboy of dime novels, 1950's television shows and Buffalo Bill's Wild West Show, have created a sartorial vocabulary that endures to this day. For the millions of children who have happily sported the suede vest with the matching skirt or chaps and hat and holster that were all the rage in the 1950's, "It was like a modern-day armor for cowboy heroes," says Art Emr. "It was the distinctive outfit that made you one of the good guys."

Today's designs often evoke a romanticized past. A number of designers make clothing that speaks to our frontier era, with band-collar shirts, vests, and wool pants. Some perpetuate western heritage by reproducing items found in museums, such as split riding skirts of leather with bone buttons. One designer's line of contemporary western clothing incorporates '50's styling, while another uses antique textiles, including vintage Beacon blankets, to make one-of-a-kind jackets. Many designers strive for an antiqued look; one says she doesn't put labels in her clothes because she'd prefer that people think they were made a century ago.

Many of today's Western fashion designers are directly inspired by their very vivid western experiences, on cattle and sheep ranches, in the rodeo stock contracting business, in the practice of ancient Native American ceremonies. But even those who handle the animals from which their materials come, or live amidst the imagery that appears on their clothes, are influenced by something that goes well beyond lifestyle. That is, they are subject to the larger enduring aura of the West, an aura born of timeless landscapes and charismatic personalities.

Whether the result is a Miss Rodeo America outfit featuring beads and crystals sewn onto leather, a western wedding gown of heavy brocaded satin mixed with beaded silks, or an engraved eighteen-karat gold buckle set for a president, it is always a direct expression of today's West. One designer says her work is "infused with Western spirit." Another says her designs spring from "my research and pleasure in all things old, and the magic of Wyoming." Yet another sees in nature "endless inspiration for design" in exquisite colors and "layers and layers of textures and dimension." One maker calls her frontier-inspired fashions, simply, "the heart of the West."

The clothing appeals for a very basic reason, says Juti Winchester. "People love to repeat the romantic aspects of the West, even 100 years later. I think for them it's a way of taking it home and keeping it. Cowboys and Indians are not people who are bound up in convention. When you can wear a piece of Western clothing, it represents freedom."

Reversible Denim Shawl and Waistwrap
Ann 'N' Eve, Anette Sarkissian, Burbank, California

93

The Cowboy Hat

A Little History

by *William Reynolds*
& *Ritch Rand*

From *the Cowboy Hat Book* by William Reynolds & Rich Rand, Copyright 1995, Photos Copyright 1995 by Banning Co. Reprinted with permission of Gibbs Smith, Publisher

Doc Carver's Stetson
The nutria fur Stetson with a Montana Peak crown and flat brim has tan grosgrain brim edging and hatband, with an added leather hatband. The hat was used by champion rifle shot and Wild West showman Doc Carver in the 1890s.
(Courtesy of the Gene Autry Western Heritage Museum)

There are few items in the history of American culture that carry the same iconic weight as the cowboy hat. It is the one item of apparel that can be worn in any corner of the world and receive immediate recognition. As the old cowboy saying goes, It's the last thing you take off and the first thing that is noticed.

The history of the cowboy hat is not that old. Before the invention of the cowboy hat (which means before John B. Stetson came along), the cowpunchers of the plains were castoffs of previous lives and vocations. Everything, from formal top hats and derbies to leftover remnants of Civil War headgear to tams and sailor hats, was worn by men moving westward.

The cowboy hat is truly an example of form following function. Invented by John B. Stetson (the son of a Philadelphia hatmaker), today's cowboy hat has remained basically unchanged in construction and design since the first one was created in 1865. As the story goes, John B. Stetson and some companions went West to seek the benefits of a drier climate. During a hunting trip, Stetson amused his friends by showing them how he could make cloth out of fur without weaving.

on to itself. As the water dries up, the fur contracts and the little prongs and hooks draw closer and closer together as additional kneading is applied.

After creating his "fur blanket," Stetson fashioned an enormous hat with a huge brim as a joke, but the hat was noted to be big enough to protect a man from sun, rain, and all the rigors the outdoors could throw at him.

Stetson decided to wear the hat on his hunting trip, and it worked so well that he continued wearing it on his travels throughout the West. Later, he sold the hat to a rugged horseman who was fascinated by the unique headwear. Stetson received five dollars for his invention, and as he stood back and watched the horseman ride

The Bonanza Boys, Michael Landon, Pernell Roberts, Dan Blocker and Lorne Greene ready for some hat-wearin' shoot-'em-up action (Courtesy of Ritch Rand)

Stetson used the fur from hides collected on the hunting trip. Kneading the fur and working it with his hands, dipping it into boiling water, spreading it out, kneading it, and dipping it again, he created a soft, smooth piece of felt. Using a technique that has been known since the beginning of modern civilization, Stetson amazed his friends by using the only material he had at hand- fur.

Fur is essentially the hair of certain mammals and is made of a series of little hooks and prongs. When stimulated by kneading and water, matting occurs, which causes the fur to hold

Hats being finished in finishing department. Brims are being sanded to a smooth finish. Circa 1930's. (Courtesy of Bailey Hats)

Nudie's Personal 5X Stetson with Rhinestone Hatband

This gorgeous off-white Stetson was personally used by Nudie himself! A beautiful 5X beaver with a triangular crease and an upturned brim, it is accented with an amazing hatband consisting of silver-colored leather with three rows of rhinestones and a small silver-toned buckle. Nudie's stamp and sticker price for hat and band appear on the sweatband. Worn by Nudie Cohn in the 1980's. (Courtesy of the Gene Autry Western Heritage Museum.)

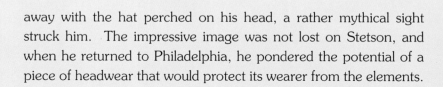

Roy Rogers
No cowboy hat book would be complete without Roy slicked up in his Bohlin belt buckles. (Courtesy of Ritch Rand.)

away with the hat perched on his head, a rather mythical sight struck him. The impressive image was not lost on Stetson, and when he returned to Philadelphia, he pondered the potential of a piece of headwear that would protect its wearer from the elements.

In 1865, as the cattle business began to boom, Stetson became convinced that the cowmen of the West would see his new hat as a useful addition to their wardrobe. He began to produce the first incarnation of his "big hats" (originally called the Boss of the Plains) in number, and immediately dispatched samples to potential dealers throughout the West. As they say, " to make a long story short," Stetson was soon inundated with orders for the unique headgear. He even attracted the attention of the Texas Rangers, which quickly became the first law enforcement group to use cowboy hats as part of its official uniform.

Wild Bill Elliot as Red Ryder in The San Antonio Kid   *(Courtesy of Ritch Rand)*

Classic Navajo Bailey

A 1970's Bailey Natani, this hat is made of pressed black felt with a high, straight-sided, domed crown and a stiff 4" brim. Around the crown is a beautiful Navajo silver hatband with a rope motif. On both sides are butterfly ornaments, and at the center, a many-petaled flower. The tips of the butterfly wings and flower petals are accented with teardrop-shaped pieces of turquoise. Stamped on the inner band is the inscription "Many Farms Trading Post, Many Farms, Arizona." This one's a classic!

(Courtesy of the Gene Autry Western Heritage Museum.)

Before long, Stetson was considered the maker of this newfangled headwear, the cowboy hat. It had the unique capability, even in those early years, to identify its wearer as someone associated with the West, and that meant the cattle industry, whether he wore cowman's gear or not. Merely by placing his new cowboy hat on his head, he became part of the growing fraternity of cowmen who carried with them an image and aura intrinsically linked to the Wild West.

The cowboy hat rapidly became a regular and necessary part of the cowman's daily wear. The wide brim made quick work of fanning a fire. It could be used to whip a horse, wave to distant riders, and yes, even lend an air of grace and prestige to the man beneath its brim. And, of course, during inclement weather, the cowboy hat served as a very effective umbrella.

Beyond its utilitarian use around the ranch, the inclination to fill the crown made the hat a perfect hiding place, as well. It became the chosen spot for hiding money and important papers that would be unprotected elsewhere. As we all know, the first thing a cowboy puts on in the morning and the last thing he takes off at night is his hat; so, it was a natural place to keep his secrets and treasures, hence the phrase "keeping something under one's hat."

Left to the imagination, the cowboy hat became a valued addition to the wardrobe of any man of the West. Because of the tight weave of most Stetson hats, the concept of the "multi-gallon" hat came into play, as it was waterproof enough to be used as a bucket. Actually, the term ten-gallon did not originally refer to the holding capacity of the hat (the average hat held only a few quarts), but to the width of a Mexican sombrero hatband, and is more closely related to this unit of measurement by the Spanish than to the water-holding capacity of a Stetson.

Then, like today, a well-made cowboy hat was not inexpensive. In fact, the cowboy hat was considered to be a major investment. The original Stetson hat sold for five dollars. Today, hats of equal quality can sell for over one hundred dollars to upwards of one thousand dollars. Before the heyday of the cowboy (between 1860 and the end of the 1880's), Stetson hats made of fine beaver sold for anywhere from ten to thirty dollars. The irony is that the hat often cost more than an entire suit of clothing, and it wasn't unheard of for a man to spend a month's wages on a hat.

Shortly after the turn of the century, the cowboy hat, although still in its infancy, nevertheless infused its wearer with a singular link to the history of the wild and woolly West. Even after

Guy Madison Wearing his Wild Bill Hickock hat.
(Courtesy of Ritch Rand.)

the "wild" aspect of the West was somewhat tamed, the cowboy hat never really lost its ability to lend that reckless and rugged aura to its wearer.

With the advent of the motion picture (and shortly thereafter, the silver-screen cowboy), the cowboy hat experienced a resurgence of popularity. Eager and impressionable audiences saw cowboy hats on the likes of Tom Mix, Bill Hart, and Ken Maynard. The romantic and rugged characters these actors portrayed helped the cowboy hat and its wearer maintain a "wild and woolly" image.

In addition, there came to be a kind of code to the particular style, shape, and size of the cowboy hat. While it remained a universal image of the American West, certain nuances in shape, size, and style provided specific information to the wearer's background and geographical base. With a subtle adjustment to the brim and a couple of extra dents in the crown, a man could indicate that he was from the northern regions of Nevada or the rough plains of Texas, the wind-whipped ranges of the Rockies or the low deserts of New Mexico.

For example, in the high-desert reaches of northern Nevada, cowboy hats take on a rugged, historic look that seems to be a merging of the vaquero of California and the cowman of Texas. The hats worn by these riders of the scrub sage tend to carry a more surreal yet conservative look; crowns tend to be more open or simply dented in on the side; brims tend to be flat. In many cases, attempts were made by ranch crews to recreate a "family crease," generally devised from the classic "cattleman three-crease" (two side creases and one top crease) with a longhorn brim, which were often found around the stockyards of Texas. It is the nature of the crease in the crown and the shape of the brim that creates a unique accent for the person wearing a particular hat. While styles come and go, crown heights and brim widths seem to vary only marginally with the passing of time.

Today, while there are many manufactures involved in making both inexpensive wool and felt machine blocked hats, as well as custom manufacturers making hand-creased magic, the basic

Dave Jones' Tan Stetson
Working cowboys in the Cody, Wyoming area favored the clothing and supplies found at Dave Jones' shop. This tan Stetson with upturned brim edges and two creases in the crown was purchased from Jones' shop and bears this message on the inside of the hatband: "Buy it of Dave Jones, Cody, Wyoming." A small steer emblem is attached to the front of the crown.
(Courtesy of the Gene Autry Western Heritage Museum)

hat remains the same. Its function continues-to protect its wearer from the blistering effects of the sun and the tortures of wind and rain. While some of today's hats remain true to their turn of the century beginnings and others follow their own design features, today's cowboy hat continues to be seen as the last vestige of apparel of a young and untamed nation. It makes a statement about the tough individuality at the center of every pioneer that carved a life from the new frontier.

Sherry Holt Reese

Desert Diva
by Sherry Holt

The fun, feminine designs of Sherry Holt Reese are the marriage of her love of Hawaii, where she spent most of her life, and Western culture. She has lived in California for the past seventeen years, and was instrumental in redefining beach culture as a fashion classic. Her *Desert Diva* line, produced by Kenco Fashion and overseen by Jenken Chang, is a lighter, more feminine version of traditional Western: classic dresses, swing skirts, vintage blouses, and cleverly shaped jackets on original fabrics, many hand-painted. Reese's fabrics of choice are denim and rayon and her trademark is practical simplicity; her clothes sell at 1,200 stores internationally. Reese has been sewing her whole life; "I started at four years old when I created a doll because my parents wouldn't buy dolls for me and my sisters." Later, she was an art major at the University of Hawaii , focusing on drawing, painting, and textile weaving. "At this time, I love doing couture, draping, sewing, and pattern-making." Today she still does couture work with her studio collection, available at Cinnabar Creek in Big Timber, Montana. Reese lives at the beach, where, she says, "Art is a way of life." She also travels, with many of her designs inspired by the flowers, cacti, cowgirls, antiques, horses, and other elements of the West that she observes on the road. A new dress design, for instance, was inspired by a lariat. "I dreamt of mixing lassos with polka dots, and chose silk organza to mix with rayon polka dots. I thought of the old movies when women looked soft, sexy, and had small waists and broad shoulders. My "Lingering Lasso" shows a Western look of long ago that is so fashionable now."

Photo: Greg Patterson

Jo Orchard

Thunder Moon

Jo Orchard moved to a cattle ranch in Wyoming 25 years ago and took up leather and beadwork shortly thereafter. Her lifelong interest in the lifestyle of the Plains Indians blossomed into a full-blown passion, and ultimately a career. A respectful student of Native American culture, she has learned techniques, built skills, and refined her perspective by reading, attending seminars, visiting museums, and immersing herself in the cultures of the nearby Wind River and Crow Reservations. She has taken part in powwows and celebrations, watched her daughter perform in a traditional dance dress and accessories of her own design, and has been honored by being asked to make celebration dresses for several Native American women. In her hands, traditional patterns are given new energy in a refreshing blend of color and fabric. Her ideas come from "living in the mountains and seeing the red cliffs and surrounding landscape change with the seasons, and seeing the colors of earth and sky blend into some of the most beautiful combinations you can imagine."

Photo: Elijah Cobb

101

Sorrell Custom Boots

Lisa Sorrell started sewing when she was twelve and took it up professionally at fifteen. Thirteen years ago she took a job in a boot shop and discovered her life's work. Since establishing her own shop, her cowboy boots have been featured in books and museum shows, have been worn by celebrity actresses and country singers, and have earned renown in a major bootmaking competition in Texas. What's distinctive about her work is not just the quality and precision of the stitching but the designs: her lively juxtapositions of colors and her imaginative subject matter. "Plain Freedom" features a one-piece top with a geometric border, inlaid with buffalo and running horses; Native American symbols decorate the wing and counter tip. Her unique designs range from remarkably intricate patterns of intertwined floral motifs or grape leaves to ranch brands, reproductions of traditional designs, and a children's rainbow-moon-and-stars pattern. What sets her boots apart, though, is their graceful shape. "I'm often told that my design ability stems from the fact that I'm female. Yet I learned design from a bootmaker named Jay Griffith, who was an ornery old cuss with a delicate flair for design. He told me that a cowboy boot should look like a 'Coke bottle or a beautiful woman,' and he'd make an hourglass shape with his hands. He's the reason I make boots with sexy, graceful lines."

Photo: Bozarth Photography

Anette M.
Sarkissian

Ann 'N' Eve

A native of England and a graduate of a design school in London, Sarkissian has been working in her craft for twenty years. Of Russian and Armenian heritage, she grew up in a family of musicians and artists and learned sewing from her mother and sister. She launched her design business in London with a line of clothes made from Italian silks and fine wool. After moving to southern California fifteen years ago, "I became fascinated by the lavish embroidery and rhinestones and fringes incorporated into western wear, especially of the old times." She cites the clothes worn by Dale Evans and Roy Rogers and designs by Nudie as important sources of inspiration. The winner of many awards and ribbons in art and craft shows, today Sarkissian loves working with suede, leather and high-quality fabrics. "My specialty lies in using semi-precious stones, as well as feathers and rhinestones. I am constantly searching for new concepts to materialize in my designs." Her best-selling design, for instance, a reversable waistwrap with fringe, was based on the traditional chap. Sarkissian's work can be seen at her store in Burbank, California, and at several Western festivals.

Photo: Karl Preston

Anne Beard

Anne Beard

A twenty-year award-winning veteran of her craft, Anne Beard grew up on a mountain ranch in Washington, and has lived in the Oregon high desert for the past ten years. The region's traditional lifestyles and her husband's family business, rodeo stock contracting, continue to "infuse [her] work with Western spirit." Designs range from elegant smoking jackets to beautifully tailored ottomans. Influenced by her mother, an award-winning fiber artist, and her brother, a custom woodworker, Beard says, "I enjoy creating diverse collections, from kitsch to serene sophistication, from definitive western to subtle insinuations." A recent project, a furniture ensemble, "is my most ambitious furniture piece to date, and a colorful homage to what I consider one of the most enduring symbols of the West, the writhing bucking horse and the battle-fatigued cowboy." It's a fitting example of her work, she says. "My work and my lifestyle are intertwined, reflective of each other."

104

Photo: DeGabriele

Hilary Smith & John Lough

Hilary Smith Company

Designer Hilary Smith has lived in Taos for almost four years; there, her work is inspired by "hiking, nature, the Taos Pueblo, and Hispanic culture." Smith has been practicing her craft for thirty years, since before she moved from England to the United States. She holds a degree from an art college in England and worked for several major knitwear companies before starting her own hand-loomed sweater company. Over the years, her designs have evolved from "contemporary fashion-forward" to concentrating on Western and Native American imagery. Her knit designs, which are made into clothing and pillows, celebrate her adopted land with such motifs as buffalo and moose, running horses and bucking horses, log cabins and pine trees, and the classic Molesworth-inspired gunfighter silhouette. Cowboy boots, spurs, revolvers, tepees, saguaro cactus, and an array of Native American imagery give definition to her work. A newly introduced piece is a full-length coat of soft, warm chenille, decorated with a hearts-and-roses graphic, crocheted flowers, and hand beading.

Photo: Kerrie Griffin

105

Julie Ewing

J. Ewing Designs

Californian fashion designer Julie Ewing is an avid gardener and sees in nature "endless inspiration for design. The exquisite colors we see in fall leaves, or a single iris, the varying blues and greens, oranges, and reds of an evening sky — the possibilities are endless. My eyes see layers and layers of textures and dimension and this gives me added inspiration." She has also been inspired by "vintage fashion designers and Paris haute couture, with their flamboyant and very detailed sense of design and their emphasis on glamour, elegance and grace." In her twelve years in Western design, Ewing has seen three Miss Rodeo Americas crowned while wearing her creations, and her work has been featured in juried shows, museums and books. Beads and crystals sewn onto leather is her favorite combination. "The intensity and scope of the colors found in beads, the reflectivity that they exude, the dimension they bring to a garment, this inspires and excites me. Looking for just the "right" antique crystals and beads to incorporate into one of my pieces is a true joy for me. As tedious and time-consuming as this can be, I believe the end result makes the effort well worth while."

Yazmhil &
Brice Corman

Bison Legacy

Yazmhil and Brice Corman's handmade products of bison leather combine a Wyoming-influenced aesthetic with the Cormans' European background. The Cormans moved from Belgium to Wyoming in the late 1980's and launched Bison Legacy in 1989; self-taught in this media, they have won awards at many fine-craft shows. Following Native American traditions, the Cormans try to complete the "circle of life" by using bison by-products as much as their creativity allows. From the first drawing through each stage of the process — designing, selecting the leather and accent materials, hand cutting, sewing, and individualizing each piece for the client — the Cormans maintain complete control of the project themselves, using no assistants or apprentices. A new piece, the Paris Charm, an evening clutch of bison leather, is suede-lined and accented with polished ivory beads. "Our lifestyle — happiness, an enthusiasm for life, the elegance and simple refinement in our craft, the beauty of nature surrounding us, good friends and good wine — is everything to us and it shows in every single piece created in our studio."

Babette Champlin
& Elda Kohls

Lillie Mae

Babette Champlin's and Elda Kohls' love for the Western lifestyle is evident in their highly original "wearable art." Their Lillie Mae vests, capes, coats, hats, shoes, and boots pay tribute to frontier styles and speak to the Victorian era. A fringed suede vest has wood beads and bone buttons. A black suede coat has a golden brown flowing inlaid design. A Victorian style hat in purple crushed velvet is embellished with a black feather spray in the front and an ostrich feather on the side, as well as chenille, ribbon, and Austrian crystals. Some fabrics are handpainted or airbrushed; some items are finished with turquoise, silver, or leaf-shaped beads of bone or wood. Both designers have an extensive background in art and interior decoration, and both have taught interior design. "Lillie Mae designs," say Champlin and Kohls, "are the heart of the West."

Janet Vitale

JVB Designs

Janet Vitale has studied her craft in educational settings from Oregon to Maine since 1975. Her work has been the subject of museum exhibits and gallery shows, and she has been honored by numerous awards and publications. Vitale makes one-of-a-kind pieces of jewelry using precious metals and precious stones through a process called die forming. This process produces smooth, clean, pillow-like and complex structural forms. The beauty and magic in die forming is in taking two-dimensional sheet metal and, by pushing and stretching, transform it into the third dimension. Her surface designs incorporate narrative symbols using the techniques of piercing, roller printing, and etching. "My art intends to illuminate the beauty I see in animals, landscapes and ancient cultures," says the artist. "I use nature's images to express myself through tactile metalwork."

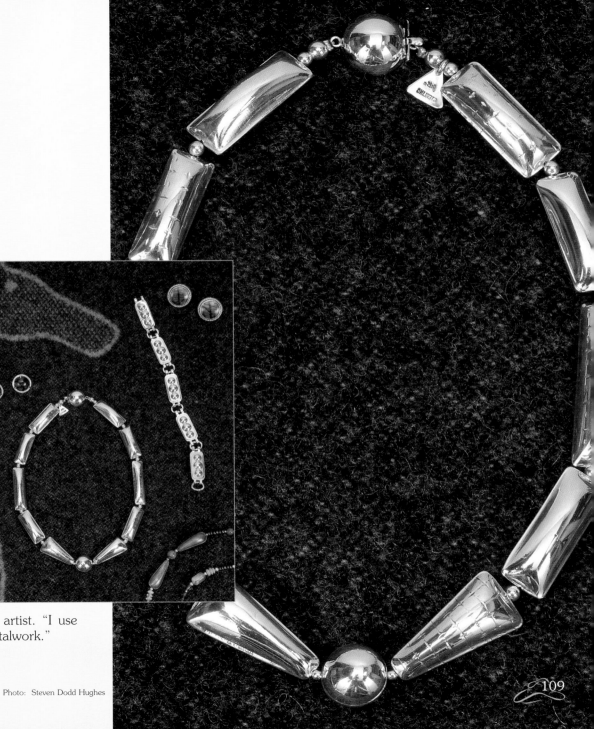

Photo: Steven Dodd Hughes

109

Pate Stetson

Women of the Wild West

Women of the Wild West was born in 1994 out of a desire to showcase Montana seamstresses, provide a second income for the struggling ranch industry, and promote true western clothing that can make the transition from ranch to city. The company began with shearling coats with handsewn appliques and reproduction riding skirts, then expanded to include jackets, shirts, skirts in velvets, linens, silks, cashmere, and wools, as well as a line of accessories: necklaces, bracelets of silver and precious beads, and hand-embroidered shawls. Clothing is often finished with locally made buttons, a bit of hand embossing, or the old-fashioned quilting stitch; many of the pieces are reproductions of originals found in museums or private collections. Founder and owner, Pate Stetson, attended the Rhode Island School of Design and worked for a number of New York fashion photographers and fashion magazines. She returned to Vermont to paint and raise horses and sheep, before marrying a Montana rancher in 1982. When she realized the resource that existed of women who worked on their ranches during the day and sewed for their families at night, her lifelong interest in fashion came full circle. Today, she says, "I'm a painter, and my husband and I ranch, so I have several lives beyond Women of the Wild West. But they all involve hands-on creativity and I am always thinking about color and form, whether it's for a painting or using material. I always have a sketchpad nearby — even in the lambing shed."

Photo: Rob Densmore

Gene Waddell & Family

Waddell Trading Company

Gene Waddell has studied and been involved with turquoise his entire life; first in the family's turquoise business in Arizona, where he was exposed to mining operations and the wholesale trade, then in the 1970s as a dealer to the top Native American jewelers, legendary artisans such as Charles Loloma, Harvey Begay, Lee Yazzie, and Mary Marie Lincoln. In 1985 he started Waddell Trading Company, a wholesaler of Native American jewelry, kachinas, baskets, and pottery, which also operates an art gallery in Scottsdale; he is part owner of Nevada's Lone Mountain Turquoise Mine. Waddell Trading Company is licensed and bonded by the Hopi tribe, represents many prominent award-winning artists, and helps up-and-coming Native American artisans by stocking otherwise unaffordable quality gemstones (ranging from semiprecious stones to diamonds) which can be incorporated into their work. "I think this jewelry is timeless," says Waddell. "It transcends trends. Besides being collected and enjoyed by people all over the United States, the Europeans and Japanese are constantly looking for quality Native American art and the finest in American turquoise. It's a privilege working with our great artists and matching their work with someone who is thrilled to own it."

111

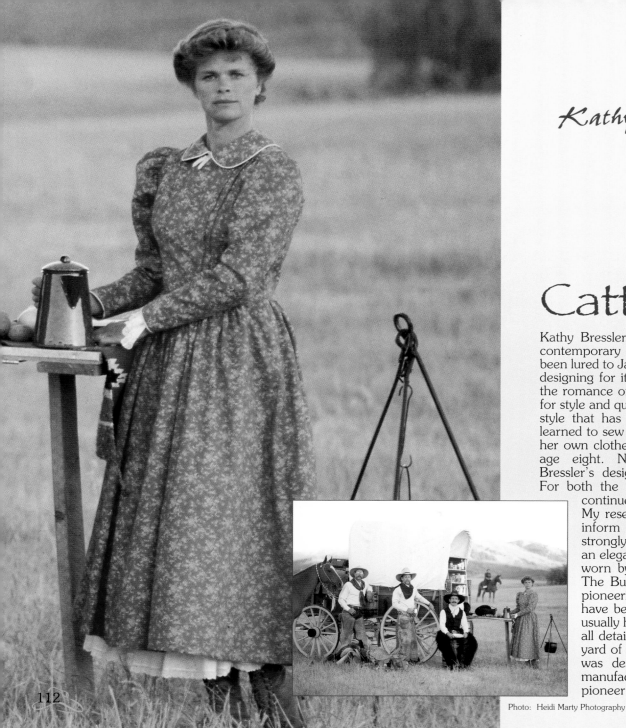

Kathy Bressler

Cattle Kate

Kathy Bressler, aka "Cattle Kate", is one of the pioneers of contemporary Western design. Twenty-one years ago, having been lured to Jackson Hole for the mountain lifestyle, she began designing for its inhabitants, especially those who appreciated the romance of the range. "We established a reputation early for style and quality, and we initiated the 'back to the Old West' style that has become popular today." As a child, Bressler learned to sew from her mother, who encouraged her to make her own clothes; she still recalls a mermaid outfit she made at age eight. Now budding seamstresses can try their hand at Bressler's designs, distributed worldwide by Simplicity Patterns. For both the patterns and her ready-to-wear line, Bressler continues to be influenced by "the magic of Wyoming. My research and pleasure in all things old inspire and inform my work." Bressler's Cattle Kate Collection strongly evokes the frontier era. "The Carriage Coat is an elegant period-style winter coat, reminiscent of those worn by fashionable ladies at the turn of the century. The Buggy Coat is a fancy duster, like those worn by pioneering women in the westward movement who may have been covered in dust. As I design a new piece, I usually have a story line to go with it. In my mind's eye, all details are complete, including chickens in the front yard of the cabin — which the Chicken Feeding Apron was designed for." Fittingly, Cattle Kate clothing is manufactured in rural America, in homage to skilled pioneer women from the past.

Photo: Heidi Marty Photography

Suzanne M.M. Warner

Elk River Beadworks

Suzanne Warner has lived in the West, including ten years in Hawaii, and has worked in the arts — as a museum professional, as a graphic designer and sign painter, in galleries and as an arts teacher — her entire life. She holds multiple degrees in art and anthropology and is Director of the Yellowstone County Museum in Billings. Thus, she brings a wealth of life experience and artistic background to her beaded creations, which are inspired by the delicate Hawaiian art of shellweaving. Her *Medicine Lodge 5*, inspired by rock art sites in Montana and Wyoming, is a beaded amulet bag with a painted pictograph image (taken from a site in the Pryor Mountains) on one side, and on the other, beaded imagery that evokes "the lovely contours and colors of the Pryors." The piece, which has a corresponding buckle, took the artist eighty hours to make. "I'm from a family of strong and talented women who all have done handwork or artwork of some kind; my mother, at 83, is still a practicing artist. I've always been influenced by nature and the anthropology, history and geology around me. I like many mediums, including photography and printmaking but spend most of my creative time doing beadweaving, as it is very time consuming. However, it is quite rewarding for me as the process involves color theory, how things fit in a space, composition and design elements in the construction that are always a puzzle. The result is for the collector, the process is for me."

Photo: Suzanne M.M. Warner

Wynd Novotny

MahVay

"I love to live on 'wild land'," says Wynd Novotny, who raises llamas on a ranch in northern California. "The forest, grasslands, hawks, owls, bobcat, and fox all influence my work and my well-being." Graduate-level work in environmental psychology "has directly influenced my desire to work with symbols that are inspired by the rich heritage of wild land and cultural diversity that is the treasure of the American West." Her *Starbird Outfit*, inspired by western swallows, "celebrates the beauty and magic of the swallow and her relationship to the night and the stars, which are essential to her ability to navigate." Made of black silk velvet, the outfit bears the Milky Way in hand sewn Swarovski crystals; a jewelry closure consists of two handsawn silver moon concho "shields" connected by a silver chain. The jacket is lined in purple silk charmeuse, with matching black velvet pants with moon concho shields on the side seams, and a matching silk charmeuse halter top. Novotny is also an artist and teacher with the International School of Metis ('Mixed') Art. "Working with the symbols and understanding which we have inherited from the meeting and mixing of the Native Americans and European immigrants who settled the West is truly inspirational. In my mixing of Chinese silk and leather is the meeting of the Chinese laborers who carved the road I live on with the cattle ranchers who herded cattle up out of Mexico and carved out their homesteads in the hills of California." In addition to her one-of-a-kind pieces, Novotny recently launched her *Folk Cultura* and *Folk Couture* lines.

Photo: Wynd Novotny

114

Cheryl Long

Pure West

For many years, Cheryl Long has used various media to capture "the West of today." Her original company, Pure West by Cheryl Long, was formed in 1989 as a garment company for the romantic cowboy or cowgirl-at-heart. Using her photographs of working ranches, she implemented classical painting techniques to romanticize her documentary photographs. These images were applied to t-shirts, home furnishings, posters, and note cards. Cheryl later created a designer level of ladies' clothing combining romantic flourishes and coloration with a vintage look. More recently, she introduced an accessory jewelry line of one-of-a-kind necklaces, bracelets, and earrings. Her collection now includes a home-decorating line of pillows and throws from hand-appliqued vintage fabrics with suedes and leather. A professional photographer since graduating from the Univeristy of Texas with a BFA in 1984, her photography has earned a spot in numerous juried shows and is represented in many corporate collections; recently her piece, "Indian Abstraction," was purchaed by the Harry Ransom Museum at the University of Texas for its permanent collection. In her clothing, she enjoys working with vintage textiles and linens, as well as deerskin, which she says is "sensuous material; you learn to work your design from the texture of the hide." More recently, she says, "I'm incorporating things like vintage Beacon blankets and other antique textiles into coats and one-of-a-kind jackets," now featured on a television series called "Vintage Revisited."

Photo: David Wesley Vaughan

Lynne Ellis-Smith

Night Bear Designs

Even as a very young child, Lynne Ellis-Smith was always attracted to the old beadwork she saw at the museums and during the Calgary Stampede. But it wasn't until nine years ago that she left her job as a systems analyst to become a fulltime beadworker and clothing designer. "I've always loved antiques and old clothes, and it seemed natural to try to recreate clothing from the past that could be worn today." Her beading lifestyle is extremely fulfilling, she says. "Since every order is different, I do a lot of research before I start to be sure I'm getting the details right. I'm fortunate to be able to learn something new with each piece, a new technique, or something about the people who wore it, and I'm proud of every one when it's finished." Ellis-Smith loves working with wild harvested hides: deer, elk, moose, especially if they're hand-tanned. Her earlier work had minimal beading, but "Now I prefer to do work where the focus is the beadwork. I have always enjoyed making pieces that look like they could have been made 100 years ago — it's why I don't put labels on any of my clothes."

Photo: John Sharpe Sharp Shots

Joel Kaye

Morris Kaye & Sons

The premier name in wholesale furs since 1935 and the largest fur manufacturer in Texas, Morris Kaye is a family business run by Joel Kaye, son of the founder. Representing the fourth-generation of his family in the fur business, Joel Kaye works with his mother, who is in charge of inventory and sales, and two sisters; one the company bookkeeper and the other runs Morris Kaye's San Antonio showroom. (There are showrooms in New York, Denver and Dallas as well.) Mink, sable, lynx, sheared beaver, fox and other specialty furs are used in a wide variety of styles including full-length coats, leather-and-fur bomber jackets, and opera capes. Morris Kaye also creates accessories ranging from hats and headbands to mink Teddy bears. A full-service operation, Morris Kaye offers monogramming, insurance, storage and repairs and will remodel old pieces. They can also create custom orders within a ten day turnaround period. Kaye says he's happy to educate new customers about fur; the company uses only the highest quality materials, and each piece comes with a lifetime guarantee. "I want them to appreciate and enjoy what they're getting," he says.

Debra Porter

Fancy Filly

A small town girl who grew up on a farm in Alabama, Debra Porter has always loved a formal affair. "I've been sewing since I was thirteen, and have made everything from dolls and purses to wedding gowns and lace shoes. Being creative is what makes me who I am. I love lace and sequins and anything fancy." After graduating in 1985 with a degree in retail and design from the University of Alabama, Porter began designing formal gowns for weddings, proms, and pageants. Ever since spending time in Texas, she says, "I've 'gone country' and discovered a new taste for Texas Style." Fancy Filly was the result of this enchantment with denim and leather. Porter's custom formal wear includes a two-piece denim and lace gown hand-beaded with sequins and pearls, and a long cocktail gown of black velvet. Her latest designs are Western wedding gowns of heavy brocaded satins mixed with fine silks with beading. Her *Home Collection* consists of a line of throw pillows with hand-woven Southwestern fabrics, accented with leather and silver nail heads. Each pillow is one-of-a-kind. She also produces Western wedding hats, and says, "I can't wait to see what happens next!"

Photo: Randal Porter

Gary D. Parsons

Hollywood Classics

"Having grown up on a horse and cattle ranch in western Oklahoma in the '50's and '60's, our roots in the West are deep," says Gary Parsons. It is this heritage that he pulls from whether he's designing saddles for the National Finals Rodeo in Las Vegas, creating belts and buckles for the Nashville music scene, or designing buckles for TV and film personalities. Past designs have included cowboy wallpaper and fabrics, belts, buckles, saddles and luggage, as well as the Tribute to the Singing Cowboy Award for the Autry Western Heritage Museum and commissions for honorees of the National Cowboy Hall of Fame. "With me, you're only limited by your own imagination," says the artist. One example is *the Ultimate Iron Horse*, a sterling silver motorcycle with hand-tooled seats and saddlebags with sterling silver and hand-laced edges. Parsons was also recently commissioned to design a buckle set with matching belt for President George W. Bush; the three-piece set is fully engraved front and back and bears a raised Presidential seal in eighteen-karat gold. "We don't rest on our accomplishments or dream about being cowboys," notes Parsons. "We are continually designing things that will be the classics of tomorrow and highly collectible in the future."

Stephen E. Sanders

Stephen's of Colorado

Stephen Sanders began his career at Revillon at Saks Fifth Avenue in New York City twenty-five years ago. He's worked with many internationally renowned designers, including Bill Blass, Halston, Adolfo, and Fernando Sanchez, in their fur and outerwear collections. After working as head of Marshall Fields' fur and outerwear collections, Sanders launched his own business. Ten years later, Stephen's of Colorado boasts retail stores in Aspen, Snowmass Village, Steamboat Springs, and Winter Park, Colorado. Sanders loves working with fur, which, he notes, is a natural and biodegradable resource, and says he is always "inspired by the West." An antique leather coat trimmed in natural Finnish raccoon and shadow fox with leather fringe, for instance, was inspired by a Western cowboy shirt. In addition to furs, shearling, outerwear, and leather, Stephen's work has also evolved into a line of accessories and home accents. "It's truly a passion," he says. "I love working with customers in my five stores and at trunk shows around the country."

Gary Anderson

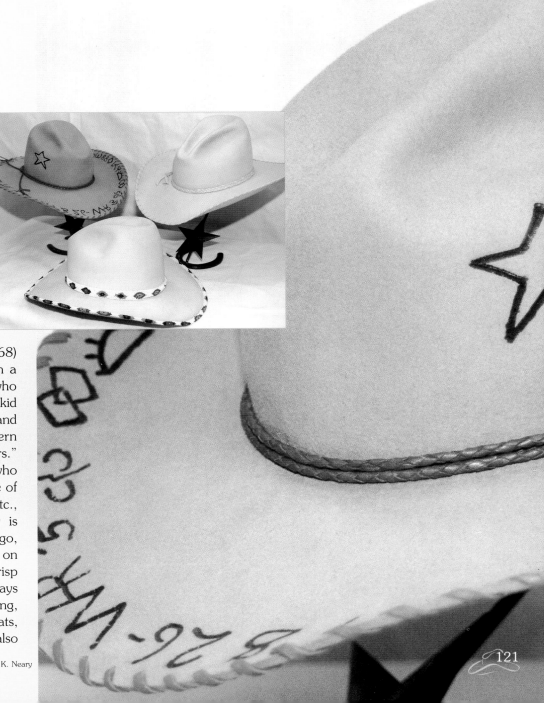

Cowboy G's & Wind River Hat Company

"Having been raised in the small town of Kirby (population 68) during the 1950's and '60's, I guess I tend to take life with a smile," says hatmaker Gary Anderson, a Wyoming native who settled in Cody ten years ago. He spent his time as a kid "fishing, swimming, cottontail hunting, cutting firewood" and listening to tales of trial and tribulation from the "Western characters of the past: ranchers, sheepherders, and coal miners." Today he spends as much time as possible with the people who actually wear cowboy hats to work, and it's a constant source of inspiration to him. "I help on ranches with calving, branding, etc., and I get to see many hat styles which some character is wearing." Since he started making hats fourteen years ago, learning his trade from a master hatter, Anderson has focused on honing the quality of his work, with finer finishes and more crisp creases. He works with imported rabbit and beaver fur, and says "starting from a raw body to a finished hat is somehow satisfying, an accomplishment of sorts." In addition to custom hats, Cowboy G's, located across from the Cody Rodeo Grounds, also offers Western wear, boots, tack, and collectibles.

Photo: Pamela K. Neary

Alan Michael

Alan Michael's USA Leatherworks

Alan Michael is known worldwide for his nostalgic fashions. He says history—from Molesworth furniture to Russian cossack uniforms — is his greatest influence. "I have always been a nostalgia buff. Everything I do is based on my interpretation of bygone eras." His rabbit-trimmed trapper coat, for instance, "is a period piece from the year 1835. Made of buckskin, the fringe work was designed to keep the elements and weather away from the body." He's also inspired by his extensive travels, and says, "I create my designs through the inspiration of cultures and people worldwide." His popular hand-tooled and inlaid vest was inspired by a pair of chaps from Spain. He favors leather and suede, and enjoys intricate tooling, inlay work, and hand-stitching. Eighteen years in the haberdashery profession in southern California have resulted in his work being seen in many movies, on television — even in the Gene Autry Museum. But his main goal, he says, is to continue to please his customers "decade after decade."

Steve Weil

Rockmount Ranch Wear

Rockmount Ranch Wear ia a three-generation family company. From its base in a historic landmark building in downtown Denver near the confluence of Platte River and Cherry Creek (where gold was discovered in 1859), the company ships its apparel, hats, and accessories to 2500 retailers spread from Santa Fe to Tokyo. President Jack A. Weil founded Rockmount in 1946 after fourteen years in the apparel industry, and has since gone on to institutionalize Western style. "He is to Westernwear what Henry Ford is to the car," say his colleagues. For instance, he introduced the first commercially made shirts with snaps, and the first commercially produced bolo ties. His son, Jack B. Weil, joined the company in 1954 and was one of the first people to introduce Western fashion to easterners. Steve Weil, representing the third generation, grew up in the business, formally joined the company in 1981, and, among other things, introduced relaxed-fit shirts, now an industry standard. Rockmount shirts have appeared in many films, such as The Horse Whisperer and The Cowboy Way, and publications. Rockmount is even represented in the Smithsonian; its signature design, with "sawtooth" pockets and "diamond" snaps, is considered the longest continuously produced shirt in the country.

Cowboys are Forever

Corral West Ranchwear & Wrangler

Founded in 1951 as the Red Lodge Trading Post in Red Lodge, Montana, Corral West has grown to be the country's largest Western wear retail chain, with 96 locations throughout the West (including Stampede Drive in Cody). From jeans and shirts to hats and boots to work wear and outerwear, Corral West is "What the West Wears." Corral West is proud to see their apparel in action in the many Western-lifestyle events that the company supports, including the National High School Rodeo Association, the National Little Britches Rodeo, the National Senior Pro Rodeo, Cheyenne Frontier Days, and the PRCA Finals Rodeo, held annually in Las Vegas.

In 1897, C.C. Hudson, at just 24 years old, was working in an overall factory in Greensboro, North Carolina, sewing on buttons for twenty-five cents a day. When the plant closed he and a few others purchased several of the sewing machines and in 1904 incorporated Hudson Overall Company. For twenty-four years, C.C. Hudson served as president of the company that ultimately grew into Wrangler, Inc. The company's emphasis changed over the years and 1947 marked a turning point with the introduction of Wrangler Authentic Western jeans. Today, Wrangler, Inc. is an international apparel giant whose brand is synonymous with the word "Western."

THE "AUTRY"

We are proud to present "The Autry"   In the summer of 2001, Scott Emmerich of The Tres Outlaw Boot Company and Tony Stanton of Sunset Trails Silversmiths, sat down over a cold beer or two to discuss their collaboration on the creation of the ULTIMATE BOOT. This boot would entail the finest skills of craftmanship that each designer could bring to this endeavor.

Produced by Scott Wayne Emmerich

Created by &
Available From:
TRES OUTLAW BOOT CO.
SUNSET TRAILS SILVERSMITHS

TRES OUTLAWS BOOT CO.
Production:
915-544-7777
fax 915-544-1606
Sales:
310-440-2577
fax 310-477-1867

SUNSET TRAILS SILVERSMITHS
909-694-1695 • fax 909-694-9946

HANDMADE *American Indian* JEWELRY

Lovena Ohl
Waddell Trading Co.

Furniture

Detail: Northwest Native Designs
Ernie & Wendy Apodaca
Snohomish, Washington

Living the West

by *Chase Reynolds Ewald*

The Old Faithful Inn, Yellowstone National Park
1998 Winner of the Cody Award

Western furniture design has evolved greatly since its stump-and-post origins a century ago. From a simple bench made of a log set across two notched log sections, to the astounding variety of work being done today, the style continues to evolve in directions which allow for new influences while in some manner holding to a traditional Western aesthetic. This evolution — which has introduced highly refined and non-indigenous woods, sophisticated metal- and wood-finishing techniques, and the fusion of disparate styles, artistic disciplines, and regional expressions — are the result of three great bursts of creative productivity over the past century. Each has driven the style forward in huge leaps, and each has broadened the audience for the genre considerably.

It is no coincidence that each major advance in productivity and design innovation has coincided with an influx of outsiders being exposed to the grandeur of the West for the first time. "The West has been one of those really inspirational places where, even if you don't live there, you're drawn to," explains Byron Price, Director of the Charles M. Russell Center for the Study of Art in the American West at the University of Oklahoma. "It is our spiritual center."

After the closing of the frontier in the 1880's, the first initial period of discovery was during the first decades of the new century. It was the era of mobility, and Americans took to the road and the rails in huge numbers. The West, with its monumental national parks and charismatic cowboys, Indians, wildlife, and scenery, was a favorite destination. Western style at that time was set by the rustic regional aesthetic typified by the great lodges of the national parks. Few people could have failed to be impressed by the soaring, monumental scale of the lobby in the Old Faithful Inn, its massive four-sided fireplace of native stone, and the rustic visual symphony created by the interplay of forked branches which comprise its dramatic tiered balustrade.

This new mobility gave birth to the dude-ranch industry, which enjoyed its golden era during the '40's and '50's. In a second burst of creative energy in Western design, cowhands became furnituremakers. They would spend the quiet months building beds, benches, dining tables, and chairs for the dudes who flocked to the scenic valleys of the Rocky

129

Bowed Cocktail Square, Chajo
Chanin Cook & Jonathan Edie, Napa, California

In 1989, the revival of interest in Thomas Molesworth, generated by a major museum exhibition, launched the current period of contemporary Western furnituremaking. This has been one in which the relentless pursuit of quality has gone hand-in-hand with a vision of the West that is broader and more reflective of the individual artisans producing the work than had been true previously. In the work of today's craftspeople, we detect their interests, passions, individual lifestyles, educational and career backgrounds, as well as wide-ranging design influences, from Amarillo to Asia, from Art Deco to Arts & Crafts, from Wild West rodeos to the history of the western pioneers.

Inherent in the new work, says Byron Price, is an expression not only of the land, but of the craftsperson who created it. "These craftsmen carry with them a lot of different baggage: their cultural setting, ancestry, training, and their set of beliefs and feelings. Western and rustic furnishings show the hand of their maker and, when done well, convey a pride of craftsmanship and artistic integrity that is translated to the user."

Mountain West each summer. From log couches to chairs made from barrels, it was a period of rough-hewn innovation and experimentation which made great use of the addition of wildlife and ranch themes to a basic rustic style. Dude ranches cultivated the first generation of ranch-owners-as-second-home buyers. From Moses Annenberg to John D. Rockefeller, these people needed furniture — lots of it — for their lodges, guest cabins, and outbuildings. In stepped Thomas Molesworth, who set up a furniture shop in Cody in 1931 and came to virtually define Western style during three highly productive decades. In his hands, applied pole, sheet-metal cutwork, and the introduction of leather, fringe, and beadwork on furnishings created a then-contemporary Western aesthetic that resonates to this day.

Whatever its manifestation, Western furniture is always born of the land. In the furniture being produced today, however, that connection may be subtle. For instance, says Byron Price, "Western furniture, done on a monumental scale, can evoke the landscape. Yet there are very delicate pieces that remind us of the little details in nature that intrigue us as well. The really good furnituremakers bring both into play — the mass and the detail."

Sundown, R.C. Hink, Bellevue, Idaho

But whether it's created from the found materials outside the door — lodgepole pine and juniper, mesquite and willow, reclaimed barnwood and old hardware, antlers, bark, and pinecones — or introduces an unprecedented level of refinement through the use of cherry or walnut with inlaid exotics, for instance, Western furniture, says Byron Price, should "stylishly and comfortably engage the West."

"I've done some Western design from an Oriental perspective," muses Wally Reber, Associate Director of the Buffalo Bill Historical Center, and a furnituremaker and artist. "But it still comes down to peeled pole, leather, and the imagery and artistry of the West. It doesn't mean you can't use different woods and fancy veneers, but it still comes down to the Western aesthetic. A cowboy boot is a cowboy boot," he points out, no matter the materials.

While it's important to show some continuity, Price suggests that the introduction of new ideas is imperative in a living art form. Contemporary Western craftspeople he says, "are both reflecting tradition and creating new avenues of expression. And I think that that is what makes it a strong, viable art. If they were simply replicating Molesworth, or rehashing stuff that's been done before in a commercial way, there's a place for that. But the tradition doesn't really live unless it's being practiced by people who are bringing something new to the table."

Both Wally Reber and Byron Price suggest that, while innovation is indeed crucial to the development of a style, the most powerful pieces are nevertheless the ones that are deeply rooted in tradition. "The best are very rich, very well-done, very beautiful — and very traditional," says Reber.

Price agrees. "The most beautiful pieces remain the most traditional. When you look at Western furniture, you still cherish those really traditional pieces, and I guess that's what speaks to our soul. Western furniture design has stood the test of time for a good reason. It speaks to our past, our heritage, and our hopes and dreams."

131

Corral Creek Sideboard 1994
Covert Workshops, Cody, Wyoming
Photo: Devendra Shrikhande

Fire started it. Imagine for a moment our ancient, cave-dwelling ancestors' lifestyle. They figured out how to harness, start, and use fire. It brought warmth and light. It offered protection from wild animals and insects, and it cooked food.

It's Friday evening and Mukmuk has just built a roaring campfire in front of his suburban cave and is ready to sizzle a saber-toothed tiger strip steak on a stick. It's been a long, hard fortnight of hunting and gathering and Mukmuk is ready for a weekend.

"Oy, my aching back," Mukmuk mutters as he leans over to barbeque his filet. Spying a nearby log that isn't on fire, he drags it closer. Mukmuk squats down on the log so that he might more comfortably hold his tiger treats over the smoky blaze.

"Ahhhh, that's better," Mukmuk sighs, wishing for a nice Merlot to go with it but France hasn't been invented yet.

That was the beginning of the rustic furniture tradition. Somebody used basic and natural elements to make a chair. That tradition continued through history as man discovered woman (a much better discovery than furniture) and woman discovered decorating.

Seriously, for generations we made our own furniture out of materials that were easily accessible. Finally craftsmen came into their own and the rest of us figured out we could have better, more comfortable furniture if we let an expert build it. Besides, we could also use the time previously spent making our own furniture to be more efficient hunter-gatherers and bankers. With the exception of isolated, rural areas where store-bought furniture wasn't easily available, furniture building became the province of trained specialists.

Cody Style

by *Thom Huge*

Reprinted from *Points West* by permission of the Buffalo Bill Historical Center

Fire at Fault

It was fire that did it. Fire started the rustic furniture movement. But before we talk about how it started, let's start with what "rustic" is and what does it have to do with cowboys?

Rustic furniture incorporates nature into its design, letting us see natural elements with little or no alteration, using the twists and turns of wood, bark, antler, horn and leather to bring form and function to the piece. The term also implies that someone without the formal training of a furnituremaker built it.

to leave treasured pieces of furniture along the trail because they were simply too heavy to ford a river or make it over a high mountain pass. Highways like the Oregon Trail were littered with everything from fancy bureaus to pianos. When the pioneers, heavy with courage but light on sofas, arrived at their varied Western destinations, they couldn't just pop in to their local discount department store to furnish their new homes. They made their own, simple furniture from materials they had at hand.

Rustic as a Style

In the 1740's we began to see designs for "tree furniture" in Europe but it wasn't until the 1st half of the 19th Century that its popularity took hold. As English families became hunter/gatherer/banker-proficient, they grew in wealth. They began to leave the cities for the suburbs and countryside. The demand began for "garden furniture." This was furniture that could be used outdoors in English gardens, supplying a comfortable place from which to enjoy the glories of nature in their private gardens. Rustic garden houses and furniture began appearing in America. Lodges and resort hotels in the Adirondacks were being built during the early 1800's as well, creating more demand for the rustic style. During the 1870's even Central Park in New York City was home to dozens of rustic structures, from cabins to gazebos.

The migration of people to the American West during the 19th Century continued the trend although for practical more than aesthetic reasons. Many a family traversing rivers and mountains of the West had

Adirondack Attack

After the Civil War, many Americans successfully pursued business careers and discovered a need to get away from it all.

Since there were no all-inclusive Caribbean resorts as yet, they began to build vacation homes in some of America's more remote locales like the Adirondacks, Catskills, Michigan's Upper Peninsula, Minnesota's lake country, the Rocky Mountains, and California. These lodges and vacation homes were being built in these areas as these areas suddenly become more accessible because these Americans were also building highways and railroads to these locales.

The Adirondacks were an especially popular retreat from the large cities of the East. Wealthy families succumbed to the charm of country summer living, getting back to nature but in a very civilized way. Let's face it, just because you, yourself, didn't cut the logs, didn't mean you couldn't enjoy the satisfying effects of sitting before an open fire.

They chose to furnish their country homes, cabins, and lodges in a manner more appropriate to the mountains and wilderness than to the city. After all, they were trying to get away from the city, albeit temporarily. They found a supply of skilled craftsmen living in the Adirondacks: carpenters and loggers who taught themselves to build furniture in their "spare time." They were talented men who built one-of-a-kind furniture.

The establishment of national and state parks in the 1890's and early 1900's gave further momentum to rustic design, construction, and architecture, as America built lodges, hotels, restaurants, and other guest accommodations in those parks.

Cowboys

The West (thought I forgot about the cowboy, didn't you?) wasn't much interested in the English gardens tradition so rustic furniture moved decidedly indoors. Western ranchers were giving life to the rustic style. As many of them discovered there might be more money in two-legged critters than in four, they converted their ranches to serving dudes.

During the long, cold winters, they often employed their ranch hands to construct furniture for the ranches. Sometimes they had to furnish an entire ranch over a single winter. These cowboys weren't formally trained but they were skilled craftsmen in their own right. They could build an entire cabin and could certainly build chairs, tables, cabinets, settees, lamps, and even beds with materials available to them on the ranches. They used logs, branches, twigs, antlers, leather, bone, and fur to make rustic though comfortable and even attractive furniture.

Teton Settee—by John Gallis
Norseman Designs West, Cody, Wyoming.

Then Came Molesworth

Cowboy style grew slowly and mostly locally. It needed a spark. That shot in the arm was Thomas Molesworth.

Molesworth was born in 1890, the son of a well-to-do preacher who moved them from Kansas to near Billings, Montana. Deciding he wanted to be an artist, Tom attended the Art Institute of Chicago in 1908–1909. Molesworth worked for a Chicago furniture company, served in the United States Marines during WWI, and then finally returned to Montana to manage a furniture company in Billings.

In 1931, married with two children, Tom Molesworth moved his family to Cody, Wyoming, and opened the Shoshone Furniture Company. The company manufactured "homemade" furniture and was, at first, a modest success.

Business took off for him two years later when Moses Annenberg, a wealthy Pennsylvania publisher, commissioned Molesworth to furnish and decorate the 10,000 sq. ft. retreat on his 700 acre ranch in eastern Wyoming. Molesworth created almost 250 pieces of furniture and decorated the entire inside of the lodge. A style was born.

Before long he was doing work for some of the finest hotels in the West. He was commissioned to design and supply furniture for a myriad of large ranches, guest lodges, and dude ranches. He was even supplying Abercrombie and Fitch so they could supply wealthy sportsmen all over the world.

Some of his earlier efforts included applying facades to already manufactured furniture but he developed his own forms, too, as he met the needs of the spaces he furnished or the materials he found. Molesworth also established relationships with Western artists whose work he incorporated into his furniture designs.

Swastika Settee ML.3.89.1 and *Swastika Chair* ML.3.89.2 — The set utilized plain and straightforward construction. The central slats and face rails are of routed hardwood selectively stained to enhance the Native American design.
Courtesy the Paul Stock Foundation, Cody, Wyoming.

He wasn't just making furniture. With his exposure to the Arts and Crafts Movement in Chicago during his student days, the Adirondack style (as evidenced by Buffalo Bill's Pahaska Tepee lodge), and his own acutely defined sense of style, Thomas Molesworth created an environment — a setting, if you will. And his influence is still felt today. From rustic to Western — from caveman to John Gallis, Mike Patrick, and dozens more like them — we see evidence of the creative spirit of man wrestling with and using what nature offers. We see the Cowboy Style.

We think Mukmuk would have been proud.

The furniture seen in this article may be viewed in the "Cody Style" Exhibit at the Buffalo Bill Historical Center in Cody, Wyoming, also home to the Western Design Conference Switchback Ranch Award winners.

William J. Betrus

Adirondack Custom Twig

William Betrus was born on the western edge of the Adirondacks Park and spent much of his childhood traveling the world as the son of a military man. "During these travels, I was exposed to many different cultures, as well as many different styles of rustic furnishings." During his high school years in New York, he was able to absorb "the richness of the surroundings of the 'Great Camps.'" Betrus favors eastern white cedar — combined with pine and birchbark and incorporating twigs and roots — for a wide variety of furniture ranging from dining sets to outdoor swings and including a remarkable grandfather clock set on a base of twisted cedar. "I can make the search for the most interesting pieces half the fun. The inspiration comes from the pieces themselves." He says, "As I look back on my many different exposures to this art form, from childhood to the present, I feel blessed that I was able to pursue my passion for them. I quite literally live my style." A lifelong outdoorsman, "from the first time I saw twig work, I knew it was for me. Growing up in the Adirondacks gave me a unique opportunity to 'breathe' rustic."

James P. White

Precision Woodworking

"I learn something from every piece I make and then incorporate that into the next piece," says master craftsman Jim White. Thirty years at his craft, plus three years working as a luthier (stringed-instrument maker) have taught him much in the way of craftsmanship, precision and the variable qualities of wood. A rolltop desk of Honduran mahogany (constructed with dovetail joints and no hardware) has purple-heart inlays and drawer pulls; a marquetry panel set into the desktop features a trout made of flamed maple, cherry, mahogany, purple heart, East Indian rosewood, ebony and white holly. A recent sofa table was inspired by its materials: reclaimed Douglas fir from an early-century firehouse in San Francisco. "The old-growth fir has a lot of character, with nail and bolt holes exposed, which adds to the charm and beauty of the piece." The table is inlaid with a scene of an early morning sunrise from the west side of the Tetons, made with ebony and coco bolo; a drawer pull made of a thick piece of ebony and left proud for a shadow effect is contoured to match the shape of the Grand Teton in the mountain range on the top. "Living in the West and pursuing many outdoor activities on both the Idaho and Wyoming side of the Tetons have influenced my work greatly. I believe that the clean, crisp air, clean streams, beauty and quiet that I enjoy in Teton Valley, Idaho, influence my furniture by crafting clean lines, yet intricate designs. I respect a life without chaos and I think my furniture represents this lifestyle well."

Photo: Brad Schwarm

Al & Cate Boswell

Pleasant Valley Furniture

Al Boswell is deeply attuned to the land on which he lives; his small farm in Missouri has been in his family for more than 100 years. "Living in the Ozarks of Southwest Missouri, my life is now blessed by the presence of trees, noble hardwoods of many species, all growing slowly, converting meager nutrients into magnificence. As a builder of rustic furniture, these trees are essential in providing both inspiration and materials of the highest quality." A veterinarian for seventeen years, Boswell was influenced by his parents, both very artistic, and his two sisters, both professional artists. Four years ago he decided on a second career as a furnituremaker and has been crafting with wood ever since. He says he tries to emphasize the natural characteristics of trees in his work. "Wood has such a great texture and feel; also, it remains a living, breathing organism." His daily life informs his work. "I live a simple life and spend lots of time outdoors with my wife and my pets, admiring nature's handiwork, which is very inspiring." A recent project, a reclining chair and ottoman, were made from mulberry wood harvested from a fence row near his home. Each piece, he says, is "constantly evaluated for the combination of beauty, solid construction, and comfort. I believe quality one-of-a-kind rustic furniture should combine poetry with purpose."

Eric Shell

"A lot of my spare time is spent exploring the country around Cody," says Wyoming native, Eric Shell. "When I'm out hiking or driving the back roads, I can't help but study the natural characteristics of the woods and think about how that wildness can be conveyed in my work." Shell learned traditional joinery and construction techniques in high school woodshop class, joined the Army after graduating, then came home to work as an apprentice and assistant to Cody furniture-maker John Gallis, where he's learned "how to take the basics and throw in a few twists. John has been really good about opening up to some of my design ideas and letting me run with them." Shell put ninety hours of work into a rocker for his brother's and sister-in-law's first baby; he combined live-edge pieces of cherry with juniper culled from the area around his parent's property. "The seat frame, crest rail, and arms of cherry and the wild juniper for the legs, rockers, and spindles give this a traditional fan-back-rocker look with a rustic Western flair." Says Shell, "I enjoy working with hardwoods like walnut, cherry, and maple but blending them with the wild woods found here in Wyoming is what really makes the pieces of furniture live. Any part of a traditional piece of furniture can be brought to life with the right piece of juniper or pine found right here."

Photo: Ron Maier Photography

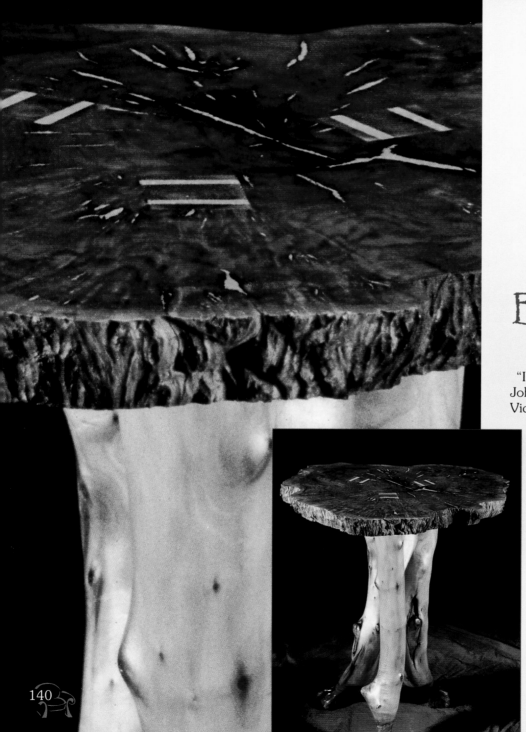

John Bettes

Bettes Woodwork

"I have been dedicated to working with wood all my life," says John Bettes. "As a child I used to be amazed by the finely carved Victorian furniture in my grandmother's house." He started working as a carpenter when he was a teenager, studied woodworking at the School of Classical Woodcarving in San Francisco and has been building furniture for the past thirteen years. "I'm inspired by the natural, diverse beauty here in western Colorado, such as the vast, open view from atop a mesa, the shadows of light from a setting sun across the arroyos, the peace and calm of floating and fly fishing the Gunnison River, and numerous varieties of wildlife in their native habitat." A recent table has a natural walnut-burl top inlaid with turquoise, with up-flowing legs anchored by traditional ball-and-claw feet. The balance of elements is what interests Bettes. "The unrefined beauty of the knots, grains, and burl are as attractive as finely carved motifs." He loves working with wood because "each piece is so unique in color, grain, and texture," he says. "I'm always inspired to see a tree destined for firewood become something lasting and useful."

Photo: Synhorst Photography

140

Michael Hemry

Michael Hemry Furniture

Michael Hemry's personal aesthetic aligns closely with to that of the Arts & Crafts Movement, a furniture style and philosophy of life that spread nationwide around the turn of the century. His chairs, tables, desks, mirrors and other pieces bear the imprints of the style with clean lines, repeating spindles in backs and sides, pinned mortise-and-tenon and through-tenon joinery, and the ebony peg details made popular in the early 1900's by the architect/designer team, brothers Charles and Henry Greene. Quartersawn white oak, a favorite of furniture-maker Gustav Stickley and his Arts & Crafts contemporaries, is still Hemry's first choice today. "It is a hard, durable wood that mellows to a golden patina with age. In quartersawn, striking patterns in the wood create immediate visual appeal." Each piece glows with a hand-rubbed finish. A woodworker for twenty years, Hemry says he wants people to enjoy living with his furniture as much as he enjoys making it. "I use the furniture I make," he says. "It's made to be comfortable, good looking and last for generations."

Photo: Elijah Cobb

141

Stacey Robinson

Chance Design

"My major influence is the land," says Stacey Robinson, "in particular the West, where my background in agriculture and landscape architecture has taught me to appreciate the land and the unique features that are so often overlooked." Working almost exclusively in steel and stone — marble, granite and travertine — and sometimes incorporating leather, Robinsons' furniture designs feature Western imagery or abstractions; the Madison console table, inspired by the Madison River, is made of cold-rolled steel tubing with Brazilian granite, accented by recycled steel plate in a dynamic fish motif. "It must be some sort of primeval thing but there is nothing better to me than to work with hot metal. The stone has its own sense of beauty and permanence." A landscape architect since receiving his degree in 1991, Robinson has been making furniture for the past couple of years and won a major landscape-architecture award for site furniture located on Main Street in Miles City, Montana. "My passion is our metal work. There is an incredible sense of satisfaction working with cold, raw materials and turning them into something that has a sense of warmth and richness."

14

Photo: Phil Bell

Dennis & MJ Judd

Big Creek Natural Form Furniture

Dennis Judd has been influenced by Native American designs, Adirondack style and Frank Lloyd Wright, but his biggest inspiration comes from nature and from the materials with which he works. Birch bark, willow, alder, and ironwood offer natural grace in form and texture, he says; in his hands they become bark-covered cabinets, bent willow loveseats, alder and willow tables with birch bark surfaces, even an unusual bent-willow "fainting couch" and a six-foot-tall grandfather clock of speckled alder, sandbar willow, and white birch bark. Judd has been building furniture fulltime since 1986; previously he worked as an airline mechanic and carpenter. He and his wife, MJ, have worked together for the past several years, building a Prairie-style house and incorporating their work with birch bark into tables, mirrors and picture frames. A new hall table called Rustic Elegance, combines planed cherry boards and a white birch bark with hand-peeled ironwood. MJ says the piece makes use of ironwood's "grace and strength, while its beautiful sinewy texture accents the natural curves."

Photo: Elijah Cobb

143

Chris Prager

Chris Prager's Chop Chop Wood Shop

A career firefighter and an artisan for the past seventeen years, Prager's love of the West was solidified during five summers working as a wrangler in Dubois, Wyoming. Over the years, his artwork has focused on wooden busts, walking sticks, totem poles and chainsaw wildlife sculptures. "Only recently have I brought my artistic and furniture-making skills together to create unique and expressive, Western-themed pieces. I am only now starting to develop and appreciate the introduction of these skills to furniture design." A nightstand hutch of white pine with oak veneer features a wood-burned horse profile on the cabinet door, an arrowhead design on the drawer fronts and, on the side panels, a cowboy on a bucking bronco, inspired by Wyoming's license plate. "I enjoy the opportunity for unique expression in both wood sculpture and furniture design. Sculpture challenges me with just one opportunity to make it all work, while every piece allows me to grow and learn more."

J. Mike Patrick

New West Furniture

A fourth-generation native of Cody, Patrick grew up on the 50,000-acre Diamond Bar and Belknap ranches, managed a cattle ranch in Kenya, and ran cattle on the family ranch in Cody before building his first piece of furniture in the early 1980's. He founded New West in 1986; it is now the largest design workshop in the region. The co-founder of the Western Design Conference cites Frank Lloyd Wright, legendary furniture designer Thomas Molesworth and his mother, artist Lucille Patrick, as his main influences. Patrick continues to be inspired by the wilderness, wildlife and lifestyle of his hometown — which he celebrates in his furniture and seeks to preserve in his environmental activism — and enjoys experimenting with various styles. New West is comprised of a small, closely knit team of a dozen people and contracts with local artists and craftsmen for painting, carving, and beadwork; Patrick has seen his vision rewarded by numerous national awards and a long list of illustrious publications. Lately he's been gratified by many commissions for public spaces, such as hotel lobbies. "Western and rustic furnishings show the hand of their maker and, when done well, convey a pride of craftsmanship and artistic integrity that is translated to the user, perhaps only subliminally, but affecting how that person feels. A return to organic forms, natural and sustainable materials and individual creativity in furnishings is a very healthy thing."

Photo: New West

145

Larry Cosens

Cream Pitcher Designs

A lifetime of travel through the West has infused Cosens' work with the spirit of the West; a longterm exposure to his parents' antique business instilled in him an appreciation for well-made, long-lasting furniture. Cosens' degree in fine arts and his background in building in different materials means he has a stong appreciation for design and is comfortable working with many different media. "Wood is my favored medium," he says, "but working with metal, leather, granite, horns, etc., gives me more design possibilities." A set of Spanish Colonial-style chairs and table (commissioned by New Mexico's State Capitol Arts Foundation and permanently residing in the capitol building in Santa Fe) was built of red oak with mortise-and-tenon joinery. A hall table and matching mirror of wood, stone, cow horns and ranch brands combine in an effect that is highly distinctive, quite refined, and very Western. A recent project involved reproducing an old Western bar. Over the past twenty years, he says, his work has evolved "from plywood to exotic woods to recycled materials. Each individual piece has changed in medium and style and I won't reproduce the same piece."

Photo: Peter Lemon

James Howard

James Howard

In addition to being a well known rustic furnituremaker, Jim Howard is also an accomplished musician, songwriter, painter, photographer, and float-plane pilot. He discovered woodworking at a young age and pursued boat building when the family moved to Florida but he found his true calling when, after completing high school, he moved to his family's camp in the Adirondacks. "The unhurried life of the region, reminiscent of our country's earlier self-sufficient times and the pristine beauty of the mountains, lakes and forests have always had a revitalizing effect on me and sparked my creativity." He traveled the country working as a carpenter but by 1980 had settled in Long Lake, New York, to build rustic furniture. Known for his work in birch-bark applique, split twig, root burl and natural woods — all collected on his own property — Howard also creates pieces with a more Western flavor. Now based in Seattle, where he flies commercial float planes, Howard produces how-to videos, passing on his knowledge to the next generation of rustic woodworkers.

Photo: Lemon & Lemon

147

Burt McDonald

McDonald Mill

"A love for Western life and Western art," says lifelong Utah resident Burt McDonald, has been shaping his work for the past thirty-seven years. Recently, McDonald was inspired by a 1950's Western scene painting to build a hutch. "It's made from alder, with reclaimed hardware, from the elk-leather-covered doors to the arrows and diamonds, to the stagecoach scene with cowboys and Indians as the centerpiece." A carver, McDonald's work is featured in the restoration of the Utah State Governor's Mansion and the LDS Nauvoo Temple. His favorite wood is alder since it's easy to carve, has nice grain, and takes stain and colors equally well. His style has evolved over the years, from Victorian to Old World to Western. His ideas, he says, come from "living and traveling the mountains and deserts of Utah, Wyoming, Idaho, Nevada, and Montana; remembering the stories, legends and myths of the Old West; and using my imagination."

Wayne Ignatuk

Rustic Woodworks

Wayne Ignatuk is known for furniture made with large "natural edge" hardwood slabs and burls, all harvested by hand from his 150-acre farm/woodlot in the Adirondacks and precisely engineered square mortise-and-tenon joinery. Growing up rebuilding and refinishing antiques with his parents exposed him to woodworking and furniture design, while an eighteen-year career as an engineer taught him how "to build strength and durability into each piece." A coffee table has a cherry base with hand-cut mortise-and-tenon joinery with walnut wedges and recessed decorative birch-bark diamonds framed with quarter-round twig. The top is made from a pair of bookmatched maple burl slabs joined along their natural edge, with a piece of curly cherry scribed to fill the gap between the two sides, two butterfly keys of curly maple tying the pieces together and a decorative dovetail spline spanning the width of the tabletop. "Design and decorative features are the result of an artistic collaboration: nature's indomitable will on the wood and my own sense of beauty. The final form is determined as much by the shapes and patterns of the material as by the whim of the designer."

Photo: Nancy Battaglia

149

M. D. Davis

Designs
of the Ancients

"I am one of those rare and fortunate people who knows from the start what their life's work is. My parents instilled in me an abiding respect for all forms of artistic expression. My formal art training made me aware of the difference between trash and treasure and the human imperative in saving the latter. Some of the rock art in the shelters I explore is better than 4000 years old. The message is still there." M.D. Davis explores rock-art sites throughout the Southwest, and painstakingly records them, even grinding her own minerals then painting, using the same methods the ancients developed, on slabs of stone. "The replication of these intriguing artworks has guided me from modest images on canvas and small stones that can be displayed on a bookshelf to wall hangings that can weigh hundreds of pounds. The desire to reveal these wonderful works of ancient art to the public has driven me to design and create useful objects of furniture, tables and consoles, stone panels for building facades and inset panels for fireplaces." A recent piece features a 400-pound slab of Tennessee cherry swirl sandstone with legs of juniper and red cedar heartwoods harvested from Davis' ranch in Oklahoma. "When all of this is done to my perfect satisfaction, the most marvelous thing of all will occur. The stone will speak to me. And then you'll see some art happening."

David A. Kalas

Frontier Manufacturing, LLC

David Kalas learned metal fabrication from his father since the two opened Frontier Manufacturing together in 1996; his father retired in 1999, but left him his "you can do it" attitude, says Kalas, who started out making accessories like candleholders and shelves but has recently embraced more challenging pieces like tables, lamps and chairs.
"My medium is metal, specifically mild steel. I like working with metal because it's pleasing to take a piece of flat, uninspired steel and cut, form, bend or twist it into a beautiful piece of art. It's also fun inventing new ways of using or incorporating metal to come up with unique, original designs." Kalas' unique ideas include cabin-shaped candle lanterns and tables which combine leather, fringe, silver conchos and metal silhouettes set against a leather backdrop. "Living in the West surrounded by its culture and history inspires me. To get ideas, I just have to look around at the people, wildlife and mountains. I don't have to resort to books or magazines; the inspiration is all around me."

Photo: Ron Maier Photography

151

Custom Furniture by Andy Sanchez

Andy Sanchez learned woodworking from his father while growing up in New Mexico; he refined his skills as a finish carpenter before launching his own business, in which he is assisted by his wife, Cheryl, and their seven children. Early on, he worked in the Southwest/ Santa Fe styles but soon began developing his own style combining Santa Fe with Mission styles, and his signature diamond-shaped plugs. In 1995, a woodcutter friend brought him a large slab of alligator juniper, a scarce and distinctive tree with bark resembling an alligator's skin; it is now his favorite medium. "Most of the pieces I use are over 1000 years old. The wood is wonderfully figured. It is most satisfying to be able to preserve this wood in furniture that will last for generations." Sanchez builds massive pieces with slabs that are often four inches thick, leaving the natural cracks in the wood and filling them with pieces of stone or marble. Since he cuts his own lumber, he is able to "bookmatch" pieces; he also uses butterfly joints and other woods such as walnut or pecan to accentuate the juniper. Sanchez says the wood itself determines the usage, such as with a six-foot-round juniper table. "The bookmatched slabs had an "S"-shaped area of rotten wood running the length of the piece. I put marble into these spaces so that it looks as if the tree grew around a vein of marble." He says, "Before, I was limited to a style. Now the wood dictates the style and function."

Best of Show
Award Winner
1994

Triangle Z Ranch Furniture

Ken Siggins' workshop sits in the shadow of Wyoming's Absaroka Mountains, in the spectacular upper valley of the South Fork of the Shoshone River. There he has been building Western furniture for close to forty years, originally for his parent's dude ranch and the guests who stayed there. "A lot of my early clients were people who came out to the ranch and wanted to take a little piece of the West home with them." Later he was sought out by the people who flocked to Cody from all over the country when Molesworth's work was rediscovered following the 1989 exhibition at the Buffalo Bill Historical Center and the Gene Autry Museum. He was influenced by his grandfather, who had made furniture for the family ranch. "It was Adirondack-influenced, posts and rails done with a draw knife." He also grew up around Molesworth's furniture and certainly absorbed its influence and sense of fun. Much of Siggins' work is classic Western furniture of logs with applied pole and burls. An award-winning foosball table pits a team of cavalry against a team of Indians, with Western scenery hand-painted on the inside walls of the game table. "We have been building the 'Western style' since 1964 and enjoying every minute of it."

Photo: Elijah Cobb

Brad Greenwood

Greenwood Designs

"To me, solid wood is tangible and real," says award-winning furnituremaker Brad Greenwood. "I find its working properties are challenging. I enjoy the natural aspects of it, the smell and the feel. I like the variety and the way species of wood have a commonality but can also be so different. I try to maintain the tree's original shape and bring to life its unusual grain patterns. When I'm working on a furniture piece, I keep the wood close to its natural form. In this way it pays homage to the history of the tree." While his forms are traditional, visual interest is added through uneven edges mimicking the natural curves of the wood; inset door panels rimmed by wood, which Greenwood distresses to mimic wormwood, then stains for contrast; the marriage of different types of wood for color highlights; the occasional miniature ladder; exposed dovetail joints; and the frequent addition of butterfly inlays across natural fissures. On each piece, the artist leaves his signature — a copper leaf inlay. A fulltime furnituremaker since 1985, Greenwood has been working with wood since he was ten. He lives with his wife, Lorraine, and their four sons in the Sierra Nevada Mountains.

Photo: Elijah Cobb

154

Jeff & Barb Murphy

Grizzly Creek Billiards, LLC

Massive, sturdy and distinctive, Jeff Murphy's billiard tables, with names like *Yellowstone, Roaring Fork,* and *Pioneer,* evoke his West. "We live up on the Grand Mesa where we have a year-round creek and are surrounded by alpine meadows, aspen and fir forests, lakes and streams, as well as orchards and vineyards." The *Elk Meadow,* an all-log table with open pockets and thick burled legs, speaks to the forests; *the Oxbow,* a timber frame table with clean lines and mortise-and-tenon joinery that features an ox-yoke-style support structure, speaks to the area's pioneer past. *The Yellowstone* has "a kind of cowboy-Victorian look," and is classically proportioned with raised log panels and recycled timbers. Murphy is a Colorado native who has rodeo'd and trained with a master farrier and blacksmith but, he says, "I knew what I wanted to do the first time I walked into a shop class at school at the age of twelve." He has been working with wood professionally since 1977, first as a carpenter, later as a furnituremaker; he built his first pool table in 1994, and holds a patent on an original leveling system. He also makes game tables, chairs and wall racks. He says he will never make more than twenty-four tables a year; he wants each one to be unique and he wants to make them all himself, from start to finish. "Every one is built right, original and as unique as the person who owns it."

Photo: Ron Maier Photography

155

Pat Olson

Pat Olson Sculpture & Furniture Art

Travelers through Grand Junction, Colorado would do well to take a detour through City Hall. There they'll see Pat Olson's life-size steel sculptures of Ute historical figures Chief Ouray and his wife, Chipeta. "Ouray was a respected leader of his people in western Colorado, at a time of increasing encroachment by whites," explains Olson. "He worked hard to make that interaction as peaceful as possible. He had exactly the same kind of experiences people who work in City Hall have. The style of the work, layers of two-dimensional stainless steel sheets arranged to make recognizable three-dimensional figures, is a subtle reminder of the saying that things are not always the way they appear and that point of view has a great deal to do with one's understanding." At times a musician, photographer, gallery owner, real-estate broker and television production manager, Olson has always been an artist; he started making studio furniture in 1990. His music and several trips to the Far East continue to inform his art. Olson's furniture, which relies heavily on sheet metal and native sandstone, is functional sculpture that plays with the challenge of crafting two-dimensional forms into recognizable three-dimensional entities. "Plate steel fits perfectly with my long-term interest in points of transition and points of view." Olson's furniture strives to be "objectively useful as well as subjectively satisfying."

Photo: Karen McClean

Chanin Cook
&
Jonathan Edie

Chajo

Chanin Cook and Jonathan Edie combined their mutual passion for furniture and design to form Chajo five years ago. "Our major influence is nature. We are interested in natural materials and showcasing them within our contemporary designs. A lot of our design ideas come from the natural world around us; we spend free time backpacking in the mountains, or roaming the north coast beaches." Their five distinct collections of limited production and custom art furniture might incorporate fossilized limestone, petrified wood, textured metals, exotic and domestic solid woods and select textiles. Part of the *Otto Collection*, their *Fishbowl* piece is a fishbowl-shaped reading table with bison hide, hardwood feet, and an inset limestone top with a fossilized fish. "We were playing with the concept of ottomans; we felt the combination of stone and leather would be interesting, and might afford us the opportunity to create something one could sit on and/or use as an occasional end table. The fossilized fish in our limestone came to the forefront, and capturing the specimens became the joke--hence, *the Fishbowl*."

Photo: Hap Sackwa

Doug Tedrow

Best of Show
Award Winner
2000

Wood River Rustics

An art major in college, Doug Tedrow has been been building furniture since 1984. He was strongly influenced by childhood vacations, "seeing totems, log cabins, pueblo dwellings, deserts, mountains, rodeos, museums and especially antiques." Today his unique furniture designs are innovative and original, while continuing to be influenced by an "old lodge" style and his lasting love of antiques. His *Stacked Log Chair, Vaquero Style*, which won the WDC Best of Show award in 2000, has an old-time look. It's built of dark log sections stacked in an outward-tapering design, with built-in ashtrays and deep brown hand-trimmed leather upholstery; there's even a hidden compartment for a bottle and glasses. His case pieces often feature intricate mosaic designs in applied twig. A distinctive style Tedrow developed uses sections of wood to form a surface that actually looks woven. "I want my pieces to look old like they're 100 years old without distressing them;" he achieves this with the finishes he uses and the styling. "I like to experiment, to come up with pieces that are unique." Over the years, he says, "I've become more of a perfectionist. Every joint has to be tight. My truck is dirty, my shop's a mess, but my furniture is perfect."

Photo: David Swift

Al Hone
&
Teresa Hone

Hone's Cabinet & Design

Brother-and-sister team Al & Teresa Hone run Hone's Cabinet & Design, which was established in 1960 by their father and grandfather. Al's teenage sons, Kalib and Kade, also work in the business. The Hones' uncle and cousin teach woodcarving classes at the shop. Al and Teresa both have backgrounds in fine art, and their creations can incorporate oil painting, stained glass, leatherwork, wood carving, and sculpture. Last year's award-winning *Majestic Moose Bar* sprang from Al's love of the Old West, specifically, old Western saloons: the big mirrors, the ornate carvings, and the detail in the designs. "We took that idea and added our love for the Rocky Mountains and wildlife where we live," says Al. "We combined this with fine art, woodworking, interior design, and modern convenience." The carved raised panels of the bar are framed with aged and twisted aspen logs; the footrail is hand-forged. The curved top of the bar has a rustic carving of a streambed, complete with moose tracks. A carved, bevelled mirror is framed with glass doors and surmounted by an arched crown molding with a mountain scene and a carved three-dimensional moose head. "Living in the West gives us lots of inspiration. The Rocky Mountains give us wildlife and the beauty of nature. The culture we live in gives Western flair and style. These inspirations can be seen in our creations."

159

Jerry L. Van Vleet

Legendary Heirloom

Jerry Van Vleet grew up in Colorado and from an early age focused his artistic talents on the design and creation of unique pieces. Today, he works from the studio on his ranch located on the Flathead Indian Reservation, between Flathead Lake and the Mission Mountains of Montana. An outdoorsman, Van Vleet's Western furniture often combines wood, iron, and rock to recreate images of nature. "I like the challenge of using several different mediums and combining them to make a well-rounded piece." He develops new ideas from the vast landscapes of the West. "Coming back from a Texas furniture show and driving through New Mexico," he said recently, "inspired my *Cactus Desk*," constructed of stone, iron and wood. His *Cattail Table*, he explains, "came from living in an area with a lot of ponds and lakes. The challenge was designing something that was made of iron, looked like natural grass and cattails, but that could be used as a functional piece of furniture." Jerry Van Vleet says his goal is to combine rugged Western artistry with total functionality in every piece he creates.

Diane C. Ross

Rustic Furniture Limited Company

Diane Cole Ross has been building furniture for more than twenty years. A native of Utah, she was originally inspired by the primitive ranch furniture she'd seen on the porches of the log cabins near Bozeman, Montana, where she was a student of range and soil science at Montana State University. She's now known for her intricate applied designs combining cowboy, Adirondack and bent willow styles with Native American imagery. Her works range from birchbark-covered bar installations to case pieces with applied pole laid in Native American-inspired patterns to graceful bent-willow chairs and benches made of branches and leather. She favors willow, birch, lodgepole pine, burl, dogwood, chokecherry, aspen and cherry, and gets most of her materials — and her ideas — from her time outdoors. "The time I spend in the saddle and on foot in the woods opens my eyes to the interaction of different species in the natural environment. I am always intrigued and amazed at the constant and subtle variety in nature, and I try to show that interconnectedness in my work."

Photo: Rick Harrison

161

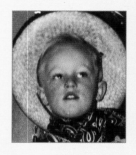

John Gallis

Best of Show
Award Winner
2001

Norseman Designs West

"I do so love working with wood," says John Gallis, a woodworker with thirty years experience and a multitude of awards to his credit. "It's such a forgiving medium to work with. Different woods are like people; they all have different characteristics and scents when you work with them, for instance, the sweet smell of cherry wood or the smooth feel of bass wood when you carve it." Influenced by Shaker and Art Nouveau styles and workshops with master woodworkers Sam Maloof, Daniel Mack and Silas Kopf, Gallis is known for meticulous craftsmanship and attention to detail, a tendency to carve edges, and a preference for curved lines over straight. His signature style employs walnut (although he also works in cherry and juniper), and positions the wood in such a way that the lighter-colored wood from the part of the tree closest to the bark forms a kind of outline for the piece. "I enjoy creating beautiful things, I start off with a pile of wood leaning against my shop wall and weeks later it's a piece of furniture that should last a lifetime." Gallis says his work has become more relaxed and less formal over the years; the award-winning *Yellowstone Desk* "had juniper legs that made the desk look as if it were moving; the walnut drawer fronts were book-matched and looked like Old Faithful erupting. I enjoy how the two woods, walnut and juniper, compliment each other." And he clearly likes the result, which he calls, "relaxed but refined."

Photo: Elijah Cobb

Christina Chapman

Best of Show
Award Winner
1998

Chris Chapman Designs

A leather craftsman for thirty years, Chris Chapman spent many years doing historical research extending back to sixteenth-century European leatherwork. Since 1974 she's been studying Native American clothing and reproducing clothing and artifacts. In 1991, she started crafting furniture incorporating leatherwork. Although she wasn't the first to apply leather to wooden frames, "Everything else I'd seen has been poorly done, because the maker's only reference had been saddlemaking. I didn't come from a saddlemaking background. I had been doing leatherwork for thirty years, been sewing since I was five and been an artist my whole life. And I had a historical frame of reference. When I started making furniture, everything I had learned before all came together." In Chapman's furniture the leather is actually shaped rather than simply wrapped around a wooden form and decorated. "The high-relief technique I've invented is like sculpting from underneath. Sometimes it's layers of leather, literally carved and sculpted and shaped, then overlaid with another piece of leather, which is worked to pull out the detail." A king-sized bed bears hand-forged iron crosses and a decorative border trim that simulates Spanish chip carving. An armoire has door panels featuring a scene with mule deer, elk, buffalo and sandhill cranes set amidst sage and Ponderosa pine with the Tetons in the background. She says, "I try to build things that will be just as appealing 100 years from now."

Photo: Dave Marlow

163

Steve Kitto

Kitto's Juniper Furniture

Steve Kitto cites his major influences as the six years spent living in an Eskimo village on the coast of the Bering Sea; long walks in the woods with his wife and dogs; and the ideas he gets from working in close collaboration with clients. "I truly love working a client's ideas into my experience with wood and design. The end result always helps me look at design from a different angle." Kitto's free-form lamps, tables, beds and other pieces are formed from Rocky Mountain, Utah and Western juniper that he says have the same appealing color, twists and deep furrows of the Alaskan diamond willow with which he first learned to make rustic furniture. He also uses pine, fir, oak and chestnut; sometimes incorporates reclaimed wood, such as old redwood railroad trestles, into his designs; and has recently been experimenting with metal and leather. Wood remains his passion, though. "The world of the self-employed wood-worker is a beautiful thing for me. I am always taking trips to the Southwest, Pacific Northwest and Alaska to hunt for interesting wood and materials for my work. I found a huge juniper tree on one of my trips to southern Utah; it was on a high exposed ridge and had been killed by a lightning strike. I struggled for over an hour to load it into my truck but I knew it would some day make an incredible desk."

164

Photo: T.K. Hill

Greg Race

Quandary Design

Quandary Design founder Greg Race is inspired by his company's setting, high in the heart of the Colorado Rockies. "Leadville has a mining and cultural heritage unmatched by any mining district in the United States," he says. "In the waning days of the eighteenth century, Leadville enjoyed a prosperity characterized by opulent decadence which brought a constant stream of prospectors, investors and outlaws to the country's highest incorporated city," (elevation: 10,152 feet). Race was a professional snowboard competitor and product tester before turning to furnituremaking fulltime five years ago. His award-winning designs utilize a variety of materials — wood, leather, glass, steel and copper (sometimes altered with heat and chemicals), as well as reclaimed items like tractor seats and fenceposts — to produce unique furniture that has a contemporary form but an antiqued, patinaed finish. "What interests me is furniture that stands on its own within an interior space," says Race. "Every piece should be able to stand by itself, should be well-designed and thoughtful and should carry its own weight."

Photo: Buffalo Bill Historical Center

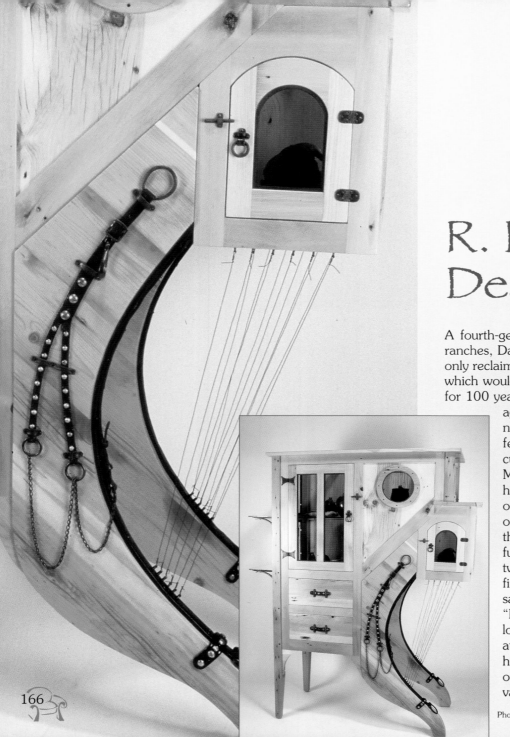

R. Dana Merrill

R. Dana Merrill Designs

A fourth-generation Idahoan who grew up spending time on his relatives' ranches, Dana Merrill adheres to a personal philosophy of re-use. He uses only reclaimed wood — fir and pine mostly — usually from neighbor's barns which would have otherwise been burnt down. "It's beautiful wood, baked for 100 years in the sun. I plane down all the old wood so it has integrity again, but there's still a patina that's baked through and the old nail holes are still there." His cabinets, sideboards, and desks feature glass-fronted compartments, woven wire racks, cubbyholes, wing-like shelves, and hooks in unexpected places. Merrill's furniture incorporates handles made from old horse harnesses and found objects such as rusty nails, harness rings, bits, old leather reins, tobacco cans, stone and scavenged wood. Each of Merrill's pieces bears a whimsical signature: wire threaded through small drilled holes and "stitched" across a crack. A full-time furniture-maker since 1993, Merrill was a contractor for twenty years before becoming a full time craftsman. He is also a fine artist and printmaker (he holds both a BFA and MFA), and says his design background adds another dimension to his work. "I think it's helped me a lot. I look at furniture as a medium. A lot of makers have classic ideas of what furniture should be. I look at what it could be." A cabinet entitled "Dana's Muse" reflected his passion for music with harp-like strings extending the length on one side. "I like my furniture to be a narrative of my beliefs, values and passions."

Photo: Dave Thompson

R.C. Hink

R.C. Hink Wood Sculptor/Artist

"I am a humorist," says R.C. Hink. "I laugh at what I create and my world seems to laugh back." Hink favors the free forms found in nature; for instance, he might use unfinished sections of tree limbs to frame a painted headboard shaped like mountains. He favors handles made of whole antlers on his case pieces. He says his favorite medium is "any wood and a paintbrush." The artist's signature creations are clearly his pieces of cowboy-boot-clad furniture. He'll carve oversized, well-used leather boots out of wood and use them as the base of the front legs of a dresser or armoire. A one-of-a-kind bench features cowboy-booted front legs, an oil painting of running horses on the back, hairy cowhide on the arms, and a carved cowboy hat and holster "draped" over the back posts. "My inspiration is all around me, from the majesty of the mountains and the natural beauty of the wilderness of the West to quite simply the footwear on my feet."

Photo: Kevin Syms

167

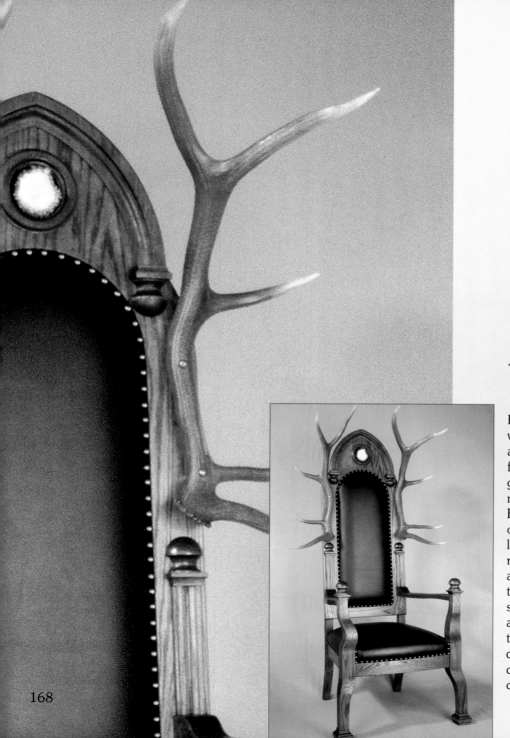

Richard Jacobi

Richard Jacobi Throne Works

Richard Jacobi has been involved with drawing, painting and woodworking professionally for forty years. He has two advanced art degrees — as well as a background in philosophy, religion, and foreign languages — and comes from a creative family. "My grandfather was a woodshop instructor; both he and my father made fine furniture in walnut and oak. My mother is an artist." His "thrones" are the product of his fascination with the melding of western and Gothic forms. In his Elk Throne, organic, twisting legs transition to antlers through its Gothic body. "An elk rosette replaces the traditional rose window in the Gothic cathedral and elk antlers radiate into space beyond the chair itself, analogous to the transcendent aesthetic of the Gothic cathedral and the aura of light surrounding western mountains. Antlers have a Western look but also have an earth-magic tradition in many cultures and lend themselves to the mythological feel of my chairs. Finials are designed to repeat forms in the antlers and the main body of the chair. The works are dark, mysterious. The monumentality of the chairs is analogous to the grandeur of the Rocky Mountain West."

Skip Odell

Odell Woodworking & Logsawing

A native easterner who studied at the prestigious Rhode Island School of Design, Skip Odell moved West thirty years ago and now lives and works in the post-and-beam home he and his wife built from Douglas fir and Ponderosa pine which they cut and milled themselves on their property high in the Colorado Rockies. More than thirty-five years of working with wood have lent a mastery to his craftsmanship, while the setting inspires his designs. "The big open spaces, wonderful colors and textures of the forests and plains, and abundant wildlife of the West generate a feeling of freedom found nowhere else." Working mostly in wood, but incorporating other materials like leather, antlers, and hand-forged hardware, he custom-designs each piece in collaboration with the client, always considering its destination and use. Odell's furniture — from an award-winning rocking chair with hand-carved ram's head arm rests, to a massive mahogany bed with tooled leather, deer hide, inlaid maple strips, and elaborately carved and colored inset panels — "starts in the imagination and is born of the materials."

169

Lynn Sedar Arambel

Ranch Willow Furniture Company

Wyoming native and rancher Lynn Arambel is one of the most original designers in the Western field; her favorite materials are aged wood, copper, willow, sheepwagons and recycled items like "primitive wood from old pickle vats, buildings, barns, tobacco sheds, antique doors and hardware, copper, stainless steel, oxidized metals — whatever blends with the piece I am working on." Her creations include a cabinet incorporating a truck door with a window that can be rolled down, and many beautifully refurbished rustic sheepwagons. Arambel learned her craft as a youngster. "My grandfather had a hunting and fishing lodge in British Columbia where I grew up during the summers. We rebuilt cabins and docks. He had no electricity and we were fifty miles from the nearest village, so we used only hand tools and materials that were readily available. We tore down old buildings and used the wood for other projects. I would go into his workshop and build things from what was left over: old wood, rusty metal, old nails that I had to straighten." From her mother, an art and art-history enthusiast, she learned about historical architecture and classic designs. Arambel lives with her husband, a third-generation Basque sheep rancher, and daughter on a ranch outside Sheridan. "Old wood is much better to use than the new woods that are being processed today," she says. "Everything is made faster and faster today, taking away from its quality. I enjoy making one-of-a-kind pieces that are thoughtfully designed and take time to create."

Photo: Kay Lynn Reilly

Hilary Heminway & Terry Baird

Best of Show
Award Winner
1994

Montana Wagons

Hilary Heminway and Terry Baird have a common love of old boards and rust. They share an ability to see potential in cast-offs and a passion for making old things new again. Heminway is a Connecticut-based interior designer who has grown up with one boot firmly planted in Montana; she attended several art academies, and has always had a passion for interiors, noting, "I think I must have started by rearranging my toys in my playpen. I've never stopped." Baird, a lifelong woodworker, owns a construction company that specializes in restoring old log buildings. Ten years ago, they collaborated to turn a derelict sheepwagon into an office space at Heminway's family's fishing camp. Since then their creations have ranged from a designer outhouse to a doghouse, from a Zen meditation gazebo to a "Snor-a-torium". Sheepwagons and wall tents are their main love, however, and in their hands these become guest houses, fly-fishing shacks, chuckwagons — eve chapels. They'll install plumbing and electricity, outfit the interior with antiques, designer fabrics, handmade hardware, and reclaimed enamelware, and attach a porch of lodgepole pine. Says Heminway, whose 2001 WDC creation was a westernized trailer, "We'll try anything."

Photo: Audrey Hall

171

Tom & Nancy McCoy

T.B. McCoy
Western Designs

Tom McCoy's furniture is highly original and resoundingly Western, inspired by Thomas Molesworth, southwestern style, old Western movies, Native American beadwork, and his own ideas. Meticulously detailed, a bed might feature leather insets, a frame might be wrapped in cowhide with rope details, conchos and burnt wood, a table might have applied pole edging, copper banding, and a ranch brand in small studs. "My work shows my love of many different mediums with wood, leather, copper, rope, glass, tacks, coins and shells. The variety is loads of fun for me. I see very little difference in how I select and approach my artwork with the mediums I use and how a painter prepares a canvas and makes use of his paints. We all have many decisions to make with many possible outcomes." McCoy has been practicing his craft for thirty-five years, and says his years of experience have taught him many ways to approach problems that might arise in the workshop. "I hope to learn something new each time I go into my shop."

Photo: Steve Buckley

172

Ernie & Wendy Apodaca

Northwest Native Designs

Wendy Apodaca is from a Montana family of ranchers, farmers, horse trainers, and cowboys. Ernie Apodaca is a Blackfeet Indian from Browning, Montana. "Our combined backgrounds influence us on a daily basis," says Wendy. In addition to five children and three grandchildren, they also share a functional-art-furniture business and gallery. Northwest Native Designs hand-builds upholstered furniture in unique designs: oversized chairs and couches, ottomans, pillows and leather throws. In addition to leather, they employ loom-state chenilles, Italian suedes, and ethnic woven fabrics. What makes their work instantly recognizable is the addition of hand-tooled leather, wood carvings that might resemble totem poles, and hand-painted Western scenes or Native American designs. "Each piece shares a story of a tribe's legends and lore," says Wendy. A club chair bears northwestern tribal designs, a wing chair is painted with a bald eagle, or perhaps a medicine wheel with horses representing the four directions. A love seat might be embellished with a design centered around peace pipes. The Apodacas have 25 years in the upholstery business, but the seven-year-old Northwest Native Designs was the result of a tragic fire. Recalls Wendy, "Inspiration came in the form of a vision to share the beauty and meaning of Native American history with others."

Photo: Mike Penney

173

Richard O'Haire

Richard's Handcrafted Furniture

A native of New Brunswick, Canada, Richard O'Haire grew up in the log cabins built by his father on the family's fishing camp, located on an island in the legendary Miramichi River. He moved to Montana at an early age, where he saw "lots of Western furniture at different ranches. This has been a real influence, and I still visit dude ranches and other places where they have old handmade furniture." For the past eight years O'Haire has been building rustic furniture of lodgepole pine and fir. A hunter and fisherman, he gathers all of his own materials in the mountains of south-central Montana. His signature touch is the addition of pinecones. "Pinecones naturally add to the rustic beauty of the piece, and bring one more beautiful part of the tree into your home."

174

Thome George

SweetTree Rustic

An avid outdoorsman, Thome George has designed and created living spaces most of his life. He began making rustic pieces in 1992. George gathers all the materials for his unique, time-intensive furniture, and has even been treed by a mountain lion in the process. While gathering the western birch that he uses for his furniture, he often taps and drinks the sweet birch water, hence the name SweetTree Rustic. "It's the forces of nature: the sun, gravity, the hill's slope, the thickness of the birch stand — all combine to create a unique group of elements. I attempt to recognize those elements as I wander through the groves, then harvest, prep, and store the wood. When I conceive of a piece of furniture, I am at the mercy of my stores. I propose a design, nature suggests a solution." He uses several species of birch, as well as serviceberry and hazel, which he may use in his signature "fringe", small twigs laid side by side extending below an edge of a piece. He also likes yew, which "has ghostlike images; it makes pine look very ordinary." Recently he's been doing fewer of his signature twig mosaics and more case pieces with solid fine-wood tops; "I like the natural salvaged edge of the tree so it's really a log slab that you're looking at. "George takes a long-term view of his furniture. "I hope I'm building pieces that will last 50 to 100 years."

Photo: Elijah Cobb

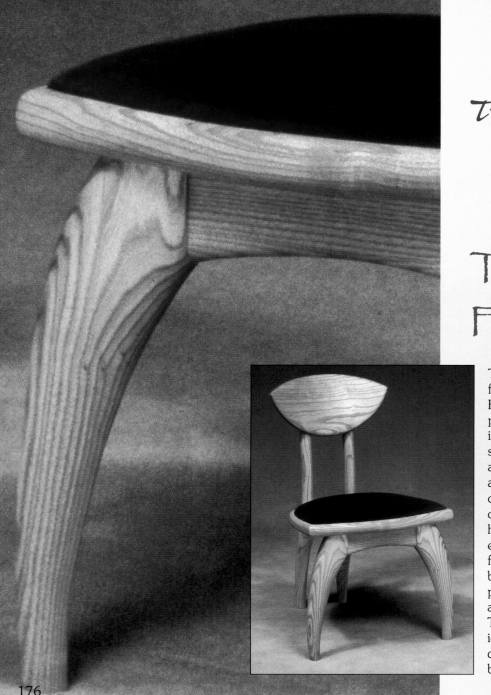

Tyler Gardner

Ty's Custom Furniture

Tyler Gardner was trained in the North Carolina tradition of furnituremaking. He earned a degree in woodworking from Haywood Community College in their intense professional crafts program, then spent seven months training under Thomas Hampson in Savannah, Georgia, before settling on the family ranch in southeastern Montana. He opened his own design studio in 1999 and has earned distinction in national venues for his very original and decidedly contemporary pieces, which include turned cherry candlesticks and an award-winning *Just Clownin' Around* chair for children. "I love the hidden beauty of wood in its raw stage. The hidden characteristics that come out in the process make the whole effort worthwhile. The touch and feel of a finely finished piece of furniture is wonderful." Gardner recently discovered the beauty of barnwood while building twenty-six interior doors. "Through the process of researching materials and making samples, I have been amazed at the natural beauty of barnwood when it has been planed. This has opened a whole new world of materials for me. I love the idea of using recycled products, putting money back in the community by buying old barns, and building and designing beautiful furniture that has a meaning and connection to me."

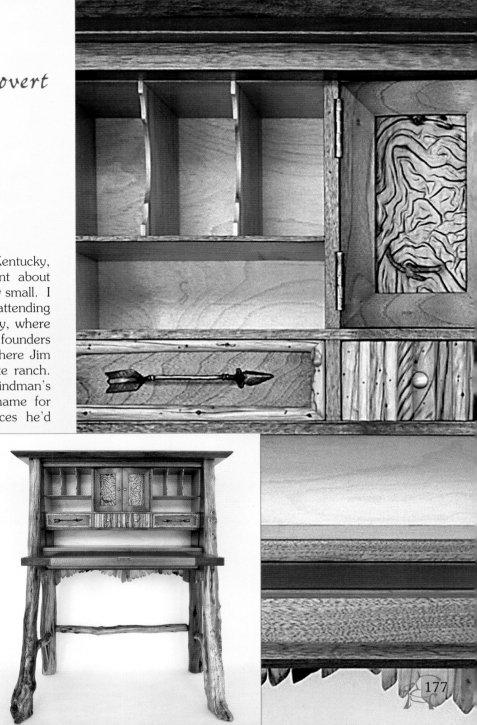

Jim & Lynda Covert

Best of Show
Award Winner
1993

Covert Workshops

Jim Covert, winner of the first Switchback Ranch Award, grew up in Kentucky, where he learned woodworking in his father's shop. "He was very lenient about letting me fool around in there with his tools, starting when I was pretty small. I built things until I went away to college when I was eighteen." After attending college in Colorado, Jim and his wife, Lynda, moved back to Kentucky, where Covert worked as a sawyer. In 1984 Covert met Ken Siggins, one of the founders of the Molesworth Revival movement; the Coverts moved to Cody, where Jim spent the next five years building furniture with Siggins on his remote ranch. By 1989 Covert had bought out old-time Cody furnituremaker Paul Hindman's shop and soon established Covert Workshops; he quickly made a name for himself with his distinctive driftwood furniture, fashioned from pieces he'd gathered along the banks of the Shoshone River. Soon, though, "I was wanting to introduce some refinement to Western furniture; I wanted to get some elegance going. So I started using cherry and walnut with driftwood and juniper." A Covert classic is a Westernized Morris chair in applied pole inset with one-of-a-kind handbeaded leather panels made by Lynda, who learned beadworking as a child in South Dakota. Other creations include a massive dining table situated atop a fantastically curved juniper stump which has been meticulously worked to bring out its color, grain and character, and an upright desk with inset leather, handforged drawer pulls and a secret drawer. Covert's work sometimes incorporates copper, antler, or brass, or carved wood or cast bronze panels by other artists. "Getting these various materials to harmonize with each other and the space and purpose to which they will be put, is extremely satisfying — when it happens. There are endless opportunities to explore."

Photo: Robert Weiglein

Mike Elliott

Mike Elliott
Western Designs

In the six years since he became a full-time furnituremaker, Mike Elliott has become known for case pieces and picture frames featuring meticulous geometric inlaid designs in undyed multi-colored woods. A bar in a restaurant, for instance, combines cedar, fir, and redwood fence rails and barn woods reclaimed from local ranches, with more than 800 individually cut pieces of naturally colored hardwood inset into its top. A barnwood armoire is decorated with 1400 willow and wild rose twigs, laid side by side to create a one-inch border, as well as 912 individually cut and inlaid triangles of naturally-colored hardwoods as the inside border. Elliott spent years working on ranches in Wyoming, Colorado, and Nevada, where he was exposed to "the rugged beauty of the West." Today, he gathers his own materials on the ranch he and his wife, Diane, bought recently in the Sierra Nevada mountains. His trademark style is influenced by the geometric patterns found in nature as well as previous work as a gemologist. "I strive for perfection in my furniture, but appreciate the irregularities, natural characteristics and unusual grain patterns in woods that serve to make my pieces unique."

Photo: Jeff Hindz

Dean Storey

Red Hill Furniture

Working from a ranch deep in the Texas hill country, Dean Storey has been making furniture for twenty years. He harvests and saws wood from dead standing trees, and crafts it into furniture with Shaker and Victorian design influences, as well as German, French, and Hispanic cultural influences. Each work is one-of-a-kind and can be inspired "from shapes found in trees, antlers shed from deer, or even an old cedar fence post." A monumental project, a front and back bar, features woods Storey acquired over the past eleven years, some from mesquite that was milled in the 1930's. "I truly enjoy getting out under a live oak tree by my shop with a grinder in hand and discovering what lies beneath the gray weathered exterior of a mesquite log. Mesquite has a character of its own, with a twisted grain pattern, cracks from the strong Texas winds, holes left by the Longhorn beetle, and burl caused by mistletoe invasion."

Photo: Dean Storey

Danial MacPhail

Best of Show
Award Winner
1997

MacPhail's Studio

Dan MacPhail raises cutting horses and Scottish Highland cattle on his farm in Kentucky, and says he's been crafting things since he was four years old. A former lobbyist and fine artist, he's been working with antlers for a decade. MacPhail burst on the Western design scene five years ago with a remarkable nine-foot-tall Christmas tree made of antlers. MacPhail's Studio crafts unique antler chandeliers, mirrors, lamps, and leather furniture. A bed with a leather head and footboard is crowned by a canopy of intertwined elk antlers; the Texas Longhorn chair has legs, arms and a back crafted from longhorns, and a seat upholstered in black-and-white cowhide. Antler is his favorite medium. Mostly he uses elk, deer, moose and sheep, but also uses some exotic imports like kudu or warthog. "I enjoy making something functional out of what was discarded by nature, and to make it aesthetically pleasing." Of his intricate, sometimes puzzle-like antler creations he says," I try to go to more trouble, more detail than anyone is willing to do. Time isn't as important as the finished piece."

Photo: Buffalo Bill Historical Center

180

Ron & Jean Shanor

Best of Show
Award Winner
1999

Wildewood Furniture

Lifelong artisans and builders, Ron and Jean Shanor are both natives of Wyoming, and it shows in their work: furniture inspired by the land and crafted from the land — with a particular fondness for the charismatic burls found in the lodgepole forests around Cody. "Ron is fascinated by all woods, of course," says Jean, "but the indigenous woods available to us in Wyoming are phenomenal. We harvest our wood sources dead and standing, but what's left over gets burned as firewood or pushed into slagpiles on the mountains when the Forest Service decides to create more habitat. This is necessary for the health of multi-use resources in forest management, and we feel that we are 'saving' the useable wood in a tasteful and functional way." The *Executive Decision* chair and desk set which captured Best of Show at the 1999 Western Design Conference, for instance, combines Russian olive, spruce, and lodgepole pine, accented by different sized burls and wormtrack. Active outdoorspeople (Ron grew up on ranches), the Shanors collect their wood on long ambling forays into the mountains and along creekbeds. "My lifestyle is fairly close to nature," notes Ron. "Therefore, my furniture designs are also."

Photo: Elijah Cobb

181

A.D. Tonnessen

Spotted Horse Studios

A.D. Tonnessen, a native of Norway, experienced the American West in college "and I've never been able to live anywhere the sky was small since." He makes furniture that evokes and celebrates his adopted land. And not just the land, he says, but "cowboys, Indians, pick-ups, wolves, buffalo, ranchers, miners, ropes, horses, cattle, mountains, clear streams, dust, wind, silver, boots, Anglos and Mexicans." A sculptor/furnituremaker who also works in stained glass, Tonnessen loves wood, especially native Texas woods, like mesquite, spalted pecan, Texas walnut and cedar. "Their solidity, color and tactile pleasures are incomparable to species of other regions. I spend a lot of time searching for special pieces of wood and in the process meet lots of great people who also have a love for the wood. In Texas, there is almost a brotherhood of people who work mesquite, and I love being a part of it." His furniture incorporates stone, silver inlays, paint and mica, and often bears hand-tooling marks. Tonnessen's furniture "should last long enough to be a source of embarrassment to your children and a thing of great value to your grandchildren and theirs."

Lester Santos

Best of Show
Award Winner
1998

Santos Furniture

An early career as an instrument-maker laid a solid groundwork for the precise craftsmanship and remarkable attention to detail found in the Adirondack and Western inspired furniture built by Lester Santos. An intimate exposure to the designs and construction techniques of legendary furniture maker Thomas Molesworth, afforded by a stint making reproductions from Molesworth antiques and Molesworth's own drawings and patterns, provided the platform for Santos' own Western design aesthetic. Today, he's primarily known for his rustic work, which is widely sought after in the Adirondacks as well as in the West. "It's very free-edge, very rustic," he says. "It's branchy and natural looking." His signature treatment may be the pieces that feature his distinctive carved woodland or mountain scenes across the drawer of a desk, for instance, or on the doors of a sideboard. Another unique Santos motif is Native American-inspired ledger-style handpainted designs on Molesworth-style chairs. Santos is a craftsman who reveres artwork found in the wild. "No one can make it better than it looks on the tree," he says.

Photo: Elijah Cobb

183

Ron & Christine Sisco

Treestump Woodcrafts

Ron and Christine Sisco have been interested in woodcraft for about thirty years, but it wasn't until both had successful careers in other fields that they turned to woodworking as a business nine years ago. They combined Ron's engineering background with Christine's passion for cooking and designed a kitchenware line: salad and pasta sets, breadboards and knives, scrapers and spoons. They've since attended hundreds of craft shows and won many awards for their work. More recently they've tried their hands at furniture, and crafted a redwood burl table. "The tree was logged over 100 years ago, and until last November, the burl was buried." The resulting four-inch-thick burl piece is almost four feet long and two feet wide in a rough oval; the Siscos left a natural edge, mounted the piece on a black walnut base, and inset the table's top and legs with turquoise for their signature look. "Our study of art history led us to a practice that the Ming Dynasty used in their pottery. They did not believe that a piece was perfect until they cracked it, then inlaid gold into the crack. For years, like most woodworkers, we tried to hide or eliminate defects in the wood. Now we look for those defects and inlay turquoise into the natural characteristics of each piece."

WELCOME *Home* . . .
TO THE QUIET *Elegance* OF WOOD.

185

Dream

Imagine

Create

Live

186

Marc Taggart & Co.
Cody, Wyoming

Photo by Dewey Vanderhoff

Built by Thomas Molesworth in the 1930s, of Inland Douglas Fir burls with hand-peeled fir legs and half rounds reupholstered in hand-painted naked German oxhide with twisted suede piping. Ottoman designed and built by Marc Taggart. Kiowa ledger art hand-painted by Chris Galusha.

Specializing in the sales and restoration of antique Molesworth furniture

◆ Reproductions

◆ Custom Designs

◆ Accessories

P. O. Box 1915
Cody, WY 82414

307.587.1800

www.marctaggart.com

e-mail: marct@wtp.net

188

WATAUGA CREEK

Home Furnishings

(800) 443-1131

(828) 369-7881 • fax (828) 524-1041
25 Setser Branch Rd, Franklin NC 28734
2 Miles South of Franklin NC on US 441
(2 Hr Drive From Atlanta)

189

Interior Design by

Robin State
Allied Member A.S.I.D.

Showroom featuring
the finest home furnishings
and representing the following
western artists:

MIKE ELLIOTT	SWEET TREE RUSTIC
CLOUDBIRD	DOUBLE D CLOTHING
LESTER SANTOS	DOUGLAS VAN HOWD
TONY ALVIS	JONATHAN SIMMONS

Sierra Design Studio

760-934-4122
www.sierradesignstudio.com

LOCATED AT 550 OLD MAMMOTH ROAD • MAMMOTH LAKES, CA 93546

Ghostrider Rustic Creations

As individual as you are

250.423.6672

Fernie BC, Canada

www.ghostridercreations.com   denise@ghostridercreations.com

Each piece designed and built by the artist

Denise Christine

Western & Lodge Furniture

RANCH RAGS

WANNA BE RANCH

COWGIRL CAFE

INTERIOR DESIGN CENTER

KUTTER RIDGE CABINS

THE GENERAL STORE

HOURS:
MONDAY - FRIDAY 10 - 6
SATURDAY 10 - 5
SUNDAY 12 - 4

Revel in Your Country's Western Heritage

5707 N. ACADEMY BLVD. COLORADO SPRINGS (719)598-4996

THE HIDEOUT

194

196

AT HOME—ANYWHERE.

John **Gallis**
NORSEMAN DESIGNS WEST

MAKER OF FINE & RUSTIC FURNITURE

38 Road 2AB ■ Cody, Wyoming 82414 ■ 307.587.7777 ■ norsemandesignswest.com

COMMERCIAL CONTRACT CUSTOM RESIDENTIAL

NEW WEST

2811 BIG HORN AVE. CODY, WY 82414
1-800-653-2391
WWW.NEWWEST.COM

WDC *Sponsor*

ROCKWELL MUSEUM
REMINGTON-RUSSELL LODGE
CORNING, NY

DOWNTOWN CODY

NEW WEST

STATE HWY. 120

BIG HORN AVENUE

NEW WEST
GUEST
HOUSE
914 RUMSEY

16th STR.

SHERIDAN AVENUE

BUFFALO BILL
HISTORICAL
CENTER

CODY CONVENTION
CENTER

17th STR.

YELLOWSTONE AVENUE

YELLOWSTONE
REGIONAL
AIRPORT

U.S. 14-16-20

199

Adirondack Rustics is Artist Owned by Barry & Darlene Gregson
Route 9 • Schroon Lake, NY 12870 • 518 532 0020 • www.adkrustics.com

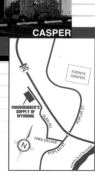

HOW THE WEST WAS WON

THEY FOUGHT HARD
THEY RODE HARD
AND THEY HAD REALLY
GOOD TASTE

PRESENTED BY

Martha Cielesz

paddysquaw@aol.com

Lifestyles

New West
J. Mike Patrick
Cody, Wyoming

The Evolution of the Rustic Movement

by *Ralph Kylloe*

I've been in the rustic furniture business for about twenty-five years now. In the early days I could walk around antique shows and flea markets and buy high-end Adirondack and "Cowboy" furniture and rustic accessories for almost nothing. At one show I purchased a really great original Molesworth three seater couch with mint condition leather upholstery for three hundred and fifty dollars. Every one I knew at the show laughed at me. I had the couch for more than a year and exhibited it and many other rustic items at several shows in the New England and New York City areas. I finally sold the couch for three hundred and ninety dollars! Demand at that time for rustic items was not high.

About twelve years ago I was invited to Atlanta to do a lecture for an interior design firm. They wanted to "push" the "rustic" look. They rented a beautiful auditorium, had it catered and spent some serious money advertising the event. With two hundred seats in the hall I was expecting a great crowd. One person showed up. I gave my lecture and slide show. At the conclusion of my show the person in the auditorium applauded and then walked out. I ate four small ham

in the hides of the animals we hunted. We articulated and expressed our lives through the natural forms that surrounded us. We gazed at the stars, marveled at the earth and learned to respect ourselves through our ability to survive against great adversity and adversaries. This way of living is hard wired into all of us.

Today we surround ourselves with plants and animals. We long to be outside when "cooped up" too long. We seem to appreciate the thunderous clouds, mountains, streams and sunrises and sunsets more then we care to admit. We crave open spaces. We marvel at wandering moose, bears, bird migrations, the great fish and dancing trees. This is from where we came. It is home to us. It is not something to be neglected. The callings of nature are not to be ignored.

Some people tell me that rustic furniture is a fad. It is not. It is a profound art form that is still under appreciated, undervalued and often misunderstood. It is not a trend. It is not a "passing fancy". It is like all things evolving.

Rustic is a way of life. It is a way of gaining meaning in our own lives. When we are troubled we usually don't go the local bowling alley or watch TV or sit in front of our computers. We seek solace sitting by the waters edge and watching sunsets. We gain strength by walking through the forests gazing at the strength of massive trees that have withstood the tests of time. We find peace in natural surroundings.

The "rustic arts" have come a long way during the past few decades. Today literally thousands "dabble" in the construction of rustic furniture. Most are hobbyists doing something they enjoy. Many are craftsmen who have acquired certain skills that allow them to create adequate pieces of rustic furnishings. And some, just a few, are artists. This last group of individuals is making a profound statement with their creations.

sandwiches, a ton of hors d'oeuvres, had a drink or two by myself then went to the airport. "Not much of a future in the rustic furniture business" I thought to myself.

But I believed in the "rustic arts". To me it was an undiscovered, under appreciated and under valued classic folk art form. Its roots were not only in regional forms of personal expression but rather the entire movement was founded through millions of generations of human evolution. We lived in caves and huts and log structures as we spread across the continents. We lived with spears, arrows and fishing tools at our side. We sat around fires each night to ward off the bugs and the beasts. We wrapped ourselves

Interest in the rustic arts seemed to spring to life about ten years ago. Prices of rustic antiques started to dramatically rise, log homes began springing up all over the country and rustic furniture builders began to finally see their creations in demand. This was also the time of the first Western Design Conference in Cody, Wyoming. I remember the conference clearly. The fashion show and dinner was held at the Ghost Town just west of town. The entire conference was fairly well attended, the furniture exhibit was excellent and the entire conference went off without a hitch. It was wonderful time.

Since that time the show has changed format and attendance has dramatically increased. Further, the uniqueness and quality of the pieces exhibited in the show has also shown considerable

improvement. Those of us who have been with the WDC since its opening days have grown a bit older and now see the show as a time to do business but also and more importantly a time to greet old friends. But equally important it is a time for growth. As we wander through the exhibits and museum we cannot help but be inspired by the creativity of others around us. The works of others influences us all. Maturation as both artists and in our personal lives happens as a result of interaction with others. That's the way the world turns.

Notwithstanding, however, it is also an opportunity for us old timers to marvel at the eagerness and creativity of some the younger exhibitors. They will no doubt replace us "older guys" with the passage of time. But us "old guys" still have a few tricks up our sleeves. No doubt Lester, Jimmy, Ron and Michael will inspire us with their latest creations and I'll be releasing a few more books that will show some of the "greatest stuff ever seen".

But if you really want to get at the heart of the show spend some time with the artists. Just about all of them will happily sit and "chit-chat" about all kinds of things. And you'll be pleasantly surprised at the conversations you'll get into. The lives of the artists are far more

complex then you realize and the life experiences of all the builders will often astound you (e.g., ask Chris Chapman what she did before she started building rustic furniture!).

The truth to the matter is that the WDC is my favorite event of the year. The fashion show is wonderful, the exhibits are awe-inspiring, the Cody area is stunning and the people are great. It is not an event to miss. I love it!

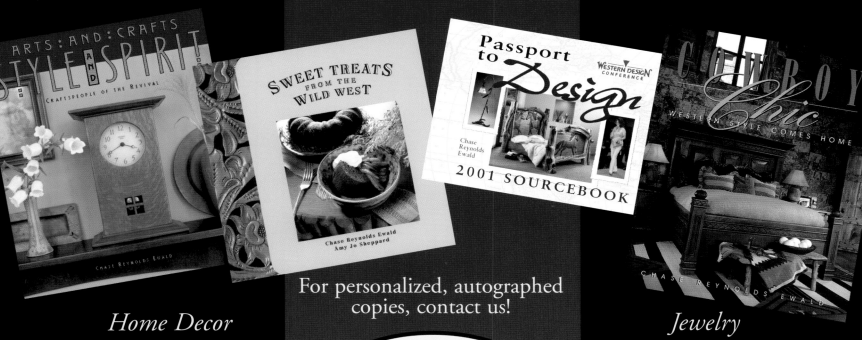

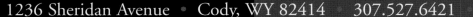

Montana Spring

The Story of One Family's Struggle to Tame a Wild New Land

Richard Magniet

A magnificent new novel based on a true story, **Montana Spring** paints a colorful picture of frontier life across the broad canvas of the Big Sky Country of Montana.

This is the story of Clay Brewer who comes west with his family at the age of eleven to carve out a new life. By the age of seventeen Clay is a U.S. Marshal and at nineteen takes a Blackfeet bride from the ill-fated tribe of Chief Heavy Runner.

Montana Spring is a story of hardship and triumph, of joy and loss, of treacherous neighbors, outlaws and renegades and the ongoing conflict between the Indians and the army. Here an unforgettable cast of characters comes to life against the rich backdrop of Montana's history as the region's pristine paradise gives way to the exploitation of her riches by trappers and traders, buffalo hunters and emigrants, miners and stockmen.

ISBN 0-9714725-1-3 $21.95

210

www.pronghornpress.org

Hard Ground 2001: Writing the Rockies
ISBN 0-9714725-0-5 $21.95

Dense Growth 2002: Writing the Pacific Northwest
ISBN 0-9714725-2-1 $21.95

A series of anthologies, published yearly with selections from Pronghorn Press' annual writing contests in which contributors focus on contemporary life in three diverse regions of the country and on the joys and perils of traveling abroad. Through poetry and prose, fiction and non-fiction, groups of talented writers share their visions of life in its most universal and also most intimate forms.

Dry Ground 2001: Writing Desert Southwest
ISBN 0-9714725-3-x $21.95

Available through your favorite bookseller or through the website!

Foreign Ground 2003: Travelers Tales
ISBN 0-9714725-4-8 $21.95
(Spring 2003)

The Place of Your Dreams . . .

Chances are, it's listed with us. Sommers & Voerding's five full-time broker owners offer over a long standing reputation of excellence and a high degree of property exposure and selection. For discreet, professional service, you can count on the real estate professionals!

www.realestatecodywyoming.com

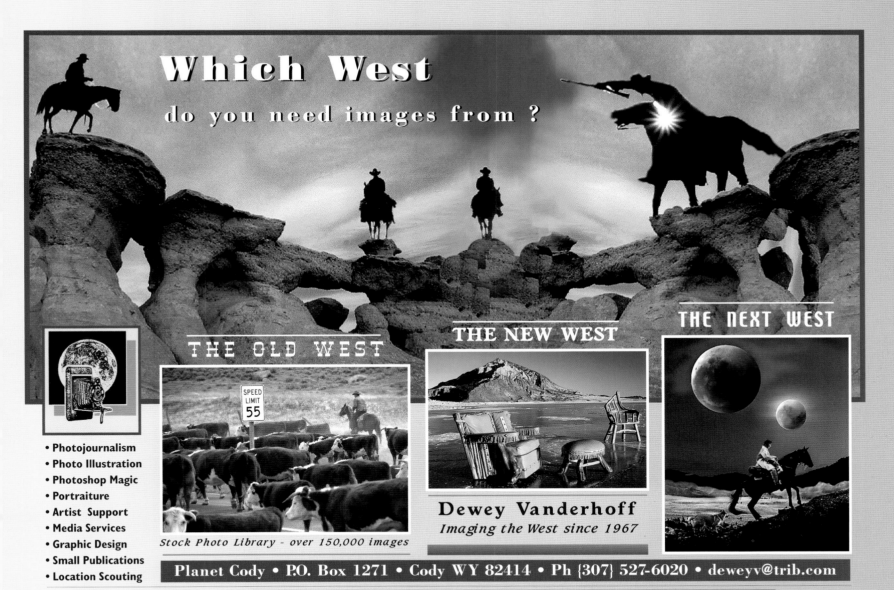

Which West

do you need images from ?

THE OLD WEST

THE NEW WEST

THE NEXT WEST

Stock Photo Library - over 150,000 images

Dewey Vanderhoff
Imaging the West since 1967

SPEED LIMIT 55

- Photojournalism
- Photo Illustration
- Photoshop Magic
- Portraiture
- Artist Support
- Media Services
- Graphic Design
- Small Publications
- Location Scouting

Planet Cody • P.O. Box 1271 • Cody WY 82414 • Ph {307} 527-6020 • deweyv@trib.com

Publisher of the Cody Boobyprise and the Cody Coyote tabloid journals

213

THE COUNTRY SUPERSTATION

KZMQ

FM 100.3
CODY-FM 101.1

104.1 FM

Classic Rock on the Eagle

Today's Hits &
Yesterday's Favorites

97.9 fm

KTAG

Big Horn Radio Network

KZMQ-FM • KODI-AM • KZMQ-AM • KTAG-FM • KCGL-FM

1400 AM

KODI
News / Talk / Sports

The Big Horn Basin's BEST Radio Stations

WDC
Sponsor

REAL COUNTRY
KZMQ
AM 1140

214

Thank you *to*
the Western
Design Conference
and Cody *for*
10 successful years
of putting
artisans *and*
buyers together.

Musical Plays • Melodrama

Cody Stage
CODY'S PREMIER THEATRE

CALL FOR UPCOMING SHOW INFORMATION,
SCHEDULES AND VENUES

CODY STAGE ■ 1110 Beck Avenue ■ Cody, Wyoming 82414 ■ 307.587.7469 ■ 888.587.SHOW

216

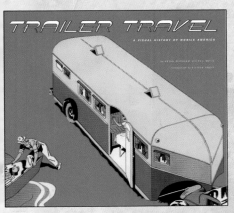

HOLLYWOOD CLASSICS

Worn by Heroes of Yesterday
Made for Legends of Tomorrow

What turns you on...

Belts
Buckles
Brief Cases
Cufflinks

Custom Jackets
Motorcycle
Conversions
Custom Designs
Upon Request

P.O. Box 333 • Fairview, OK 73737 • (580) 227-4307 phone / (580) 227-2400 fax
www.classicshollywood.com

KC Montgomery Advertising© 580-227-2206

We at Hollywood Classics believe that each piece, whether worn with denim jeans and boots or a black tie ensemble, should be something that the wearer feels the pride of ownership that goes into each piece. We use 16 & 18 gauge Sterling and fine Silver along with 14K or 18K Gold upon request.

The hand-engraved backs of the buckles, loops, and tips add that finished look to each piece. When the customer picks up the buckle to examine it, they see the care and craftsmanship that goes into our products.

The Movie Cowboys of the early days made the three piece buckle set popular and it has become a tradition carried on from the ranches to Wall Street. Growing up in the '50's & '60's our heroes were Movie Cowboys. The Wall Street moguls are fast becoming the legends of tomorrow.

Whether riding the range in an office building today and gathering cattle on the ranch lands, we believe our belts, buckles, and accessories will fit the bill.

WDC
Sponsor

Even the flamboyant Mister Dali wanted to capture the spirit of the west.

In Europe, enthusiasm for the «western way of life» is booming. Western riding, music, fashion, films, travel... all are experiencing an unparalleled growth.

Western Magazine mirrors this explosion of interest. It is distributed in two languages: a German edition for Germany, Austria, Italy, Luxembourg and Switzerland; and a French edition for France, Belgium and Switzerland.

Western Magazine brings the American West to readers all over Europe. With evocative images and original texts, it displays the richness and variety of this unique tradition.

Let Western Magazine open the doorway to the «Old World» for you.

East meets West

The Premier European Western Magazine

Western Magazine, Route de Fontvieille, 13150 Tarascon, France. Phone: Int.+ 33 490 546 985. Fax: Int.+ 33 490 546 267. e-mail: western.magazine@wanadoo.fr - www.western-magazine.com

18th Annual

JACKSON HOLE
FALL ARTS FESTIVAL
Celebrating Art in the Tetons

SEPTEMBER 6-15, 2002

Just Another Day In Paradise ©2002 Tim Tanner   Sponsored by the Jackson Hole Chamber of Commerce

Come to the
Jackson Hole Fall Arts Festival &
enjoy many significant art & cultural
events including:
Palettes & Palates Gallery Walk
Chefs On The Square
Takin' It To The Streets
8th Annual Quick Draw Art Sale & Auction
Western Visions: Miniatures and More
Arts for the Parks Exhibit and Banquet
plus many other special events.

For a festival brochure featuring a complete
listing of special events, or to order your
Commemorative Posters please call
307.733.3316

www.jacksonholechamber.com

WESTERN DESIGN
CONFERENCE

*Proud Sponsor of the 2002
Jackson Hole Fall Arts Festival*

The Western Design Institute

The Western Design Institute exists to support the School of Western Design in the United States and internationally, including but not limited to education through seminars, workshops and private instruction. The Institute will provide support for the continuance of the art of Western Design.

The Western Design Conference

The Western Design Conference exists to educate, to provide economic opportunities and to allow for the exchange of ideas, which perpetuate the best traditions of Western Design and craft.

Board of Directors

Officers

President	Vice-President	Secretary-Treasurer
Roger Murray	Kendall Siggins	Clay Johnson

Members at Large

Kay Clark   Bill Feeley   Ann Friedly   Bonnie Keeshin

John Muecke   Keith Pryor

Staff

Executive Director
Pam Neary

Executive Assistant
Gwen Fordham

2002 Sourcebook Directory

Those whose work fits in multiple categories will have additional symbols

Page 11

Mountain Living Magazine
SPONSOR
7009 S. Potomac
Englewood, CO 80112
888-645-7600
Fax: 303-397-7619
www.mountainliving.com

Page 12

Cody Country Chamber of Commerce
836 Sheridan Avenue
Cody, WY 82414
307-587-2777
Fax: 307-527-6228
www.codychamber.org

Page 13

American Cowboy Magazine
SPONSOR
P.O. Box 820
Buffalo, WY 82834
307-684-8600
Fax: 307-684-8634
sbales@cowboy.com
www.cowboy.com

Page 14

Wyoming Travel & Tourism
Michell Phelan
214 W. 15th Street
Cheyenne, WY 82002
800-458-6657
307-777-3400
Fax: 307-777-2838
mphela@state.wy.us
www.wyomingtourism.org/culture

Page 15

True West Magazine
SPONSOR
P.O. Box 8008
Cave Creek, AZ 85327
888-687-1881
Fax: 480-575-1903
usmarshal@worldnet.att.net

Page 16-17

Park County Travel Council
Claudia Wade
P.O. Box 2454
Cody, WY 82414
307-587-2297
Fax: 307-527-6228
pctc@codychamber.org

Page 18-19

Buffalo Bill Historical Center
720 Sheridan Avenue
Cody, WY 82414
307-587-4771
www.bbhc.org

Art, Accents & Accessories

Page 44

Dave LaMure Jr. Art Studios
Dave LaMure Jr.
3307 E. 3200 N.
Kimberly, ID 83341
208-736-0845
Fax: 208-733-5845
www.northrim.net/dlamure

Page 48

Cash Metals
John & Kerry Cash
2803 Bighorn Avenue
Cody, WY 82414
307-587-2449
Fax: 307-527-6840
cashmetl@wavecom.net
www.cashmetal.qpg.com

Page 49

Antler Art of the Plains
Larry Glaze
9313 County Drive 175
Carthage, MO 64836
417-358-0753
Pager: 800-201-0745
ljglaze@4state.com
www.antlerartoftheplains.com

Page 89

David Woods Cowboy Enterprises
David Woods
P.O. Box 285
Wapiti, WY 82450
307-272-0090
619-977-4049
www.historicalstagecoach.com

ADDITIONAL RESOURCES

Cowboy and Country Girl Ranch
C. Carley
650-348-1756
carley@cowboyandcountrygirlranch.ws
www.cowboyandcountrygirlranch.ws

Traditions West
Mary Lou Bunting
1131 Sheridan Avenue
Cody, WY 82414
307-587-7434
Fax: 307-587-7435
mlbunt@trib.com

FASHION

Page 90

Spirit Ware
Angela DeMontigny
Six Nations of the Grand River
RR # 6
Hagersville, Ontario NOA 1HO
CANADA
888-220-9273
wares@6-nations.com

Page 100

Desert Diva by Sherry Holt
Sherry Holt Reese
17421 E. Gale Avenue, Suite A
City of Industry, CA 91748
Contact: Jenken Chang
626-581-8881
Fax: 866-KENCO-88
slrdiva@cox.net
www.kencofashion.com

Page 101

Thunder Moon
Jo Orchard
3833 RD 82
Ten Sleep, WY 82442
307-366-2496
Phone & Fax: 307-366-2494
belgians@tctwest.net
www.tensleepwyoming.com/thundermoon

Page 102

Sorrell Custom Boots
Lisa Sorrell
217 East Oklahoma Avenue
Guthrie, OK 73044
405-282-5464
Fax: 405-282-5773
lisa@customboots.net
www.customboots.net

Page 103

Ann 'N' Eve
Anette M. Sarkissian
916 West Burbank Blvd., Suite F
Burbank, CA 91506
818-846-2033
800-834-5777
Fax: 818-767-3210
annneve@annneve.com
www.annneve.com

Page 104

Anne Beard
64209 Meadowbrook Road
Lexington, OR 97839
541-989-8144

Page 105

Hilary Smith Company
Hilary Smith & John Lough
705 Valverde Street
Taos, NM 87571
505-751-7233

Page 106

J. Ewing Designs
Julie Ewing
304 S. Rabe
Fresno, CA 93727
559-453-1678
jewingdesigns@aol.com
www.j-ewingdesigns.com

Page 107

Bison Legacy
Yazmhil and Brice Corman
10 Sage Drive
Cody, WY 82414
307-587-4199
bisonlegacy@vcn.com
www.bisonlegacy.com

Page 108

Lillie Mae
Babette Champlin & Elda Kohls
P.O. Box 43
Loveland, CO 80539
970-226-5762
Phone & Fax: 970-622-9655
elda@verinet.com

FURNITURE

Page 177

Covert Workshops
Jim & Lynda Covert
2007 Public Street
Cody, WY 82414
Phone & Fax: 307-527-5964

Page 178

Mike Elliott Western Designs
Mike Elliott
P.O. Box 2465
Gardnerville, NV 89410
530-495-1069
info@westernfurniture.net
www.westernfurniture.net
www.mountainfurniture.com

Page 179

Red Hill Furniture
Dean Storey
Route 1, Box 32A
 Mountain Home, TX 78058
830-640-3305

Page 180

MacPhail's Studio
Danial MacPhail
P.O. Box 489
1645 McKendree Church Road
Kevil, KY 42053
270-488-2522
Fax: 270-488-2523

Page 181

Wildewood Furniture
Ron & Jean Shanor
P.O. Box 1631
Cody, WY 82414
307-587-9558
Fax: 307-527-7247
www.wildewoodfurniture.com

Page 182

Spotted Horse Studios
A.D. Tonnessen
202 Barsana Avenue
Austin, TX 78737
512-394-9961
ad@spottedhorsestudios.com
www.spottedhorsestudios.com

Page 183

Santos Furniture
Lester Santos
P.O. Box 176
2120 Sheridan Avenue
Cody, WY 82414
Phone & Fax: 307-527-4407
888-woodguy
info@santosfurniture.com
www.santosfurniture.com

Page 184

Treestump Woodcrafts
Ron & Christine Sisco
P.O. Box 170
Tumacacori, AZ 85640
520-398-9123
Fax: 520-398-3939
info@treestumpwoodcrafts.com

Page 185

Bromley Construction & Log Homes
Mike & Linda Bromley
81 Whitney
Cody, WY 82414
307-587-5010
Phone & Fax: 307-587-9301
mbromley@wtp.net

Page 186

How Kola
Tim & Tiffany Lozier
507 16th Street
Cody, WY 82414
Phone & Fax: 307-587-9814
howkola@wavecom.net
www.howkola.com

Page 187

Elegantly Twisted
Randy E. Holden
17 East Dyer Street
Skowhegan, ME 04976
207-474-7507

Page 188

Marc Taggart & Company
Marc Taggart
P.O. Box 1915
Cody, WY 82414
Phone & Fax: 307-587-1800
mtaggart@wtp.net

Page 203

Martha J. Cielesz
4721 Brookview
Rockford, IL 61107
815-397-4201
paddysquaw@aol.com

ADDITIONAL RESOURCES

The Rainbow Trail Collection
John & Pam Mortensen
P.O. Box 746
Wilson, WY 83014
307-733-1519
Fax: 307-733-5216
mortensen@rmisp.com
www.rainbowtrailcollection.com

LIFESTYLES

Page 209

Chase Reynolds Ewald
77 Mount Tiburon Road
Tiburon, CA 94920
415-789-9108
Fax: 415-789-8628
crewald@sprintmail.com

Page 210

Pronghorn Press
P.O. Box 40
Shell, WY 82414
307-765-2979
pronghorn@tctwest.net
www.pronghornpress.org

Page 211

Sommers & Voerding
1025 12th Street
Cody, WY 82414
307-587-4959
Fax: 307-587-2884
svre@trib.com
www.realestatecodywyoming.com

Page 212

Blair Hotels
SPONSOR
1701 Sheridan Avenue
Cody, WY 82414
307-587-5555
Reservations: 800-527-5544

Page 213

Planet Cody
Dewey Vanderhoff
P.O. Box 1271
Cody, WY 82414
307-527-6020
deweyv@trib.com

Page 214

Big Horn Radio Network
SPONSOR
Roger Gelder
1949 Mountain View Drive
Cody, WY 82414
307-578-5000
rgelder@bhrnwy.com

Page 215

First National Bank & Trust
SPONSOR
1507 8th Street
Cody, WY 82414
307-587-3800

Page 216

Cody Stage
1110 Beck Avenue
Cody, WY 82414
307-587-7469

Page 217

Gibbs Smith Publisher
SPONSOR
P.O. Box 667
Layton, UT 84041
800-748-5439
www.gibbssmith.com

Page 218

Hollywood Classics
See Page 119

Page 219

Western Magazine
Eldorado Ranch
Route De Fontvieille
13150 Tarascon
FRANCE
011 33 490 546-985

Page 220

Jackson Hole Falls Arts Festival
Celebrating Arts in the Tetons
September 6-15, 2002
P.O. Box 550
Jackson, WY 83001
307-733-3316
Fax: 307-733-5585
events@jacksonholechamber.com
www.jacksonholechamber.com

ADDITIONAL RESOURCES

AmericInn Lodge & Suites
Joe Asay
508 Yellowstone Avenue
Cody, WY 82414
Phone & Fax: 307-587-7716
americinn@180com.net
www.americinn.com

Best Western Sunset
1601 8th Street
Cody, WY 82414
800-528-1234
Fax: 307-587-9029
www.bestwestern.com

Horse Creek
Deb Hayber
1236 Sheridan Avenue
Cody, WY 82414
307-527-6421
800-390-6305
horsecreek@vcn.com
www.horsecreekonline.com

KTVQ
SPONSOR
P.O. Box 2557
3203 3rd Avenue North
Billings, MT 59103
406-252-5611
Fax: 406-252-9938

Rendezvous Royale
Diane Ballard
836 Sheridan Avenue
Cody, WY 82414
888-598-8119
307-587-5002
Fax: 307-527-6228
art@codychamber.org
www.rendezvousroyale.org

Rustic Spirit
P.O. Box 680490
Park City, UT 84068
866-649-4799
Fax: 435-649-4024
info@rusticspirit.com

Snyder Design Group
Patti Snyder
1224 Avenue F
Billings, MT 59102
406-245-0785
Fax: 406-245-8526

Tim Wade's North Fork Anglers
1107 Sheridan Avenue
Cody, WY 82414
307-527-7274
flyfish@wavenet.com
www.northforkanglers.com

1919 Movie Poster Detail
Courtesy of the
Gene Autry Museum of
Western Heritage

Photo: Susan Einstein

235

INDEX

WESTERN DESIGN CONFERENCE